HAMLYN ALL COLOUR
SLIMMING
COOKBOOK

HAMLYN ALL COLOUR
SLIMMING
COOKBOOK

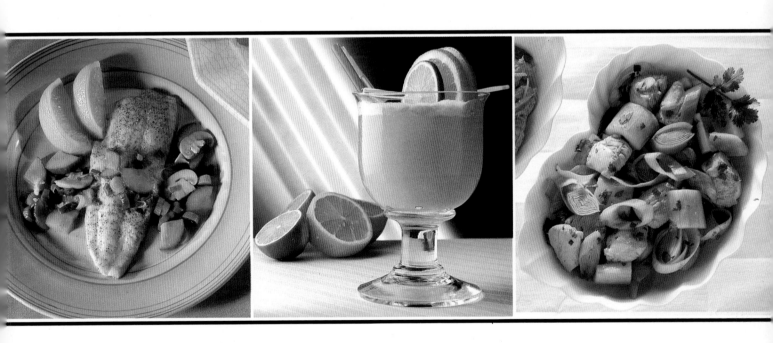

HAMLYN

Front cover shows, from left:
Plaice with Cucumber (49), San Francisco (261),
Chicken and Leeks (141).

Back cover shows, clockwise from top left:
Orange Winter Salad (181), Avocado with Raspberry Vinaigrette (25)
Cutlets with Tarragon (97), Spiced Carrot Soup (1),
Spiced Pears (229).

First Published in Great Britain 1990
by Hamlyn, an Imprint of Reed Consumer Books Limited
Michelin House, 81 Fulham Road, London SW3 6RB
and Auckland, Melbourne, Singapore and Toronto

Reprinted 1993

Copyright © 1990 Reed International Books Limited

Line drawings by Gillie Newman

A catalogue record of this book is available from the British Library

ISBN 0 600 57904 2

Produced by Mardarin Offset
Printed in China

OTHER TITLES IN THIS SERIES INCLUDE

Hamlyn All Colour Entertaining
Hamlyn New All Colour Cookbook
Hamlyn All Colour Vegetarian Cookbook
Hamlyn All Colour Indian Cookbook
Hamlyn All Colour Chinese Cookbook
Hamlyn All Colour Salads

CONTENTS

USEFUL FACTS AND FIGURES

NOTES ON METRICATION

In this book quantities are given in metric and Imperial measures. Exact conversion from Imperial to metric measures does not usually give very convenient working quantities and so the metric measures have been rounded off into units of 25 grams. The table below shows the recommended equivalents.

Ounces	Approx g to nearest whole figure	Recommended conversion to nearest unit of 25	Ounces	Approx g to nearest whole figure	Recommended conversion to nearest unit of 25
1	28	25	9	255	250
2	57	50	10	283	275
3	85	75	11	312	300
4	113	100	12	340	350
5	142	150	13	368	375
6	170	175	14	396	400
7	198	200	15	425	425
8	227	225	16(1lb)	454	450

Note

When converting quantities over 16 oz first add the appropriate figures in the centre column, then adjust to the nearest unit of 25. As a general guide, 1kg (1000 g) equals 2.2 lb or about 2 lb 3 oz. This method of conversion gives good results in nearly all cases, although in certain pastry and cake recipes a more accurate conversion is necessary to produce a balanced recipe.

Liquid measures

The millilitre has been used in this book and the following table gives a few examples.

Imperial	Approx ml to nearest whole figure	Recommended ml	Imperial	Approx ml to nearest whole figure	Recommended ml
1/4	142	150 ml	1 pint	567	600 ml
1/2	283	300 ml	1 1/2 pints	851	900 ml
3/4	425	450 ml	1 3/4 pints	992	1000 ml (1 litre)

Spoon measures

All spoon measures given in this book are level unless otherwise stated.

Can sizes

At present, cans are marked with the exact (usually to the nearest whole number) metric equivalent of the Imperial weight of the contents, so we have followed this practice when giving can sizes.

Oven temperatures

The table below gives recommended equivalents.

	°C	°F	Gas Mark		°C	°F	Gas Mark
Very cool	110	225	1/4	Moderately hot	190	375	5
	120	250	1/2		200	400	6
Cool	140	275	1	Hot	220	425	7
	150	300	2		230	450	8
Moderate	160	325	3	Very hot	240	475	9
	180	350	4				

NOTES FOR AMERICAN AND AUSTRALIAN USERS

In America the 8-fl oz measuring cup is used. In Australia metric measures are now used in conjunction with the standard 250-ml measuring cup. The Imperial pint, used in Britain and Australia, is 20 fl oz, while the American pint is 16 fl oz. It is important to remember that the Australian tablespoon differs from both the British and American tablespoons; the table below gives a comparison. The British standard tablespoon, which has been used throughout this book, holds 17.7 ml, the American 14.2 ml, and the Australian 20 ml. A teaspoon holds approximately 5 ml in all three countries.

British	American	Australian
1 teaspoon	1 teaspoon	1 teaspoon
1 tablespoon	1 tablespoon	1 tablespoon
2 tablespoons	3 tablespoons	2 tablespoons
3 1/2 tablespoons	4 tablespoons	3 tablespoons
4 tablespoons	5 tablespoons	3 1/2 tablespoons

AN IMPERIAL/AMERICAN GUIDE TO SOLID AND LIQUID MEASURES

Imperial	American	Imperial	American
Solid measures		Liquid measures	
1 lb butter or		1/4 pint liquid	2/3 cup liquid
margarine	2 cups	1/2 pint	1 1/4 cups
1lb flour	4 cups	1/4 pint	2 cups
1 lb granulated or		1 pint	2 1/2 cups
caster sugar	2 cups	1 1/2 pints	3 3/4 cups
1lb icing sugar	3 cups	2 pints	5 cups
8 oz rice	1 cup		(2 1/2 pints)

NOTE: WHEN MAKING ANY OF THE RECIPES IN THIS BOOK, ONLY FOLLOW ONE SET OF MEASURES AS THEY ARE NOT INTERCHANGEABLE.

INTRODUCTION

The Hamlyn All Colour Slimming Cookbook is packed with imaginative, calorie-counted recipes to help you lose weight by following a sensible balanced diet. It is wise to consult your doctor as to the number of calories you should have every day to ensure that you lose weight safely. This depends on several factors such as sex, age, height and lifestyle.

A colour photograph illustrates each recipe, showing how visually appealing low-calorie dishes can be. You should always aim to make food look as tempting as possible since this will encourage you to develop a preference for a healthy pattern of eating. You will then find it easier to maintain your correct weight.

Even if you like to eat your main meal in the evening, it is important that you reserve some of your calorie allowance for breakfast and lunch. This also helps you to resist any temptation to nibble during the day.

Try to plan your meals in advance so that you can be sure you have the right ingredients available and do not find yourself having to eat fattening snacks. Treat this book as if it were a menu and pick out combinations of dishes that both appeal to you and total the requisite daily number of calories.

Many slimmers still need to cook meals for other people and naturally do not want to prepare different food for them. The recipes in this book have been carefully chosen so that you can enjoy the same food as your family and friends. If you decide, however, to make a dish that is relatively high in calories, offset this by not having a second course yourself or by choosing one with few calories.

While most people realize that a recipe containing a lot of double cream would be calorie-laden, they may not perhaps know that nuts, for instance, are also high in fat. Therefore the amount of calories in a particular dish may surprise you. Gram for gram, fat contains almost twice the calories of proteins and carbohydrates. Although polyunsaturated fats such as vegetable oils are now generally considered healthier than saturated fats such as cream, both are equally high in calories.

Some fat is, of course, necessary in a healthy diet, but most people tend to eat too much. By using non-stick pans you can easily reduce the amount of fat you use or use the grill instead of the frying pan. Natural low fat yogurt makes delicious sauces and salad dressings. You will find that many of the recipes combine fruit or vegetables with fish, meat or poultry for main course dishes, which cuts down the proportion of fat.

You should be realistic about the time it may take you to reach your target weight. It is much better to do this gradually by keeping within your daily calorie allowance rather than skipping meals. In this way you will not only lose weight but also gain vitality.

With 268 recipes to choose from, dieting need never be dull.

FOOD VALUE TABLE

(In most cases, figures have been rounded up or down for ease of calculation)

Food	KJ/calorie Per 25 g/1 oz or 25 ml/1 fl oz	KJ/calories per 100 g/4 oz or 120 ml/4 fl oz
Anchovies	190/45	750/180
Apples		
raw	40/10	170/40
dried	270/65	1090/260
juice	40/10	170/40
Apricots		
raw	20/5	80/20
dried	210/50	840/200
canned	125/30	500/120
Artichokes		
globe	20/5	80/20
Jerusalem	20/5	80/20
Asparagus		
fresh	20/5	80/20
canned	12/3	50/12
Aubergine - raw	20/5	80/20
Avocado	270/65	1090/260
Bacon - lean, no fat	270/65	1090/260
Bamboo shoots	40/10	170/40
Banana	60/15	420/100
		(average size)
Bean - raw		
French	8/2	35/8
runner	20/5	80/20
broad	60/15	250/60
butter	100/25	420/100
chick peas	100/25	420/100
haricot	100/25	420/100
red kidney	100/25	420/100
Bean sprouts	16/4	65/16
Beef		
lean, no fat	250/60	1000/240
steak	230/55	920/220
minced	250/60	1000/240
stewing	250/60	1000/240
Beetroot - raw	40/10	170/40
Blackberries - raw	40/10	170/40
Blackcurrants - raw	40/10	170/40
Bread		
wholemeal	250/60	1000/240
Breakfast cereals	380-440/ 90-105	1500-1700/ 360-420
Bream - raw	100/25	420/100
Broad beans	60/15	250/60
Brussels sprouts - boiled	20/5	80/20
Butter	880/210	3510/840
Buttermilk	40/10	170/40
Cabbage		
raw	20/5	80/20
red	20/5	80/20
Carrots		
raw	20/5	80/20
canned	20/5	80/20

Food	KJ/calorie per 25 g/1 oz or 25 ml/1 fl oz	KJ/calorie per 100 g/4 oz or 120 ml/4 fl oz
Cauliflower - raw	20/5	80/20
Celery - raw	8/2	35/8
Cheese		
Camembert	355/85	1420/340
Cheddar	420-500/ 100-120	1670-2000/ 400-480
cottage	125/30	500/120
curd	170/40	670/160
Danish Blue	420/100	1670/400
Edam	355/85	1420/340
Emmenthal	460/110	1840/440
full fat soft	520/125	2090/500
Gouda	355/85	1420/340
Gruyère	500/120	2000/480
Lancashire	420/100	1670/400
Mozzarella	400/95	1590/380
Parmesan	500/120	2000/480
processed	80/90	1500/360
Ricotta	290/70	1170/280
Sage Derby	460/110	1840/440
St Paulin	380/90	1500/360
Stilton	540/130	2170/520
Cherries		
raw	40/10	170/40
canned	80/20	330/80
Chicken		
meat only, no skin	125/30	500/120
poussin	80/20	330/80
Chicory - raw	12/3	50/12
Clementine	40/10	210/50
		(average size)
Cod - raw	80/20	330/80
Cod roe - smoked	125/30	500/120
Cornflour	420/100	750/180
Courgettes	12/3	50/12
Crab - boiled	145/35	585/140
Cranberries - raw	16/4	65/16
Crayfish - shelled	125/30	500/120
Crispbread	380-420/ 90-100	1500-1670/ 360-400
Cucumber - raw	12/3	50/12
Damsons - raw	40/10	170/40
Dates - dried	250/60	1000/240
Duck - meat only, no skin	250/60	1170/280
Egg	each	
(depending on size)	170-250/40-60	
Endive	12/3	50/12
Figs		
green, raw	40/10	170/40
dried	250/60	1000/240

Food	KJ/calorie per 25 g/1 oz or 25 ml/1 fl oz	KJ/calorie per 100 g/4 oz or 120 ml/4 fl oz
Flour		
plain	420/100	1670/400
wholemeal	400/95	1590/380
Fruit juices		
apple	40/10	170/40
grape	80/20	330/80
grapefruit, unsweetened	40/10	170/40
lemon	8/2	35/8
orange, unsweetened	40/10	170/40
pineappple, unsweetened	60/15	250/60
Gelatine	400/95	1590/380
Gooseberries	20-40/5-10	80-170/20-40
Grapes	80/20	330/80
Grapefruit - fresh	12/3	50/12
		(½ portion)
Greengage - raw	60/15	250/60
Haddock		
fresh	80/20	330/80
smoked	80/20	330/80
Hake	80/20	330/80
Halibut	100/25	420/100
Honey	330/80	
Ice cream	190/45	750/180
Jam	310/75	1250/300
Jelly - made with cubes	80/20	330/80
Kipper	330/80	1340/320
Lamb - lean, raw	210-290/ 50-70	840-1170/ 200-280
Leeks	20/5	80/20
Lemon - raw		20/5
		(average size)
Lentils - boiled	125/30	500/120
Lettuce	12/3	50/12
Low-fat spread	420/100	1670/400
Lychees - raw	80/20	330/80
Macaroni - raw	420/100	1670/400
Mackerel		
fresh	270/65	1000/240
smoked	380/90	1500/360
Margarine	920/220	3680/880
Marrow	12/3	50/12
Melon	20/5	80/20
Milk, cow's		
one pint	80/20	330/80
sterilized	80/20	330/80
long life	80/20	330/80
skimmed liquid	40/10	170/40
powered skimmed	420/100	1670/400
Mushrooms	8/2	35/8
Nectarines - raw	60/15	250/60
		(average size)
Nuts		
almonds	670/160	2680/640
brazils	730/175	2930/700
cashews	650/155	2590/620
hazelnuts	460/110	1840/440
peanuts	670/160	2680/640
walnuts	630/150	2500/600
Oatmeal - raw	480/115	1920/460
Offal		
brain, boiled	170/40	670/160
heart, raw	145/35	585/140

Food	KJ/calorie Per 25 g/1 oz or 25 ml/1 fl oz	KJ/calories per 100 g/4 oz or 120 ml/4 fl oz
kidney, raw	100/25	420/100
liver, raw	190/45	750/180
sweetbread, raw	170/40	670/160
tongue	230/55	920/220
Olives	100/25	420/100
Olive oil	1045/250	4200/1000
Onions	20/5	80/30
Oranges	40/10	170/40
Parsnips	60/50	250/60
Peaches - fresh	40/10	170/40
Peanut butter	730/175	2930/700
Pearl barley - raw	420/100	1670/400
Pears - fresh	60/15	250/60
Peas	80/20	330/80
Pheasant	250/60	1000/240
Pineapple - fresh	60/15	250/60
Pigeon	270/65	1090/260
Plaice	100/25	420/100
Plums - raw	40/10	170/40
Pork - lean, raw	210/50	840/200
Potatoes		
boiled	100/25	420/100
mashed	145/35	585/140
baked	125/30	500/120
roast	190/45	750/180
chips	290/70	1170/280
Prunes, dried	170/40	670/160
Rabbit - raw	145/35	585/140
Radishes	20/5	80/20
Raisins	290/70	1170/280
Raspberries	20/5	80/20
Redcurrants - raw	20/5	80/20
Rhubarb - raw	8/2	35/8
Rice - raw	440/105	1760/420
Salmon	210/540	840/200
Sardines - drained	250/60	1000/240
		(average size)
Skate	80/20	330/80
Sole	80/20	330/80
Soya beans	480/115	1920/460
Spinach	20/5	80/20
Spring greens	12/3	40/10
Spring onions	20/5	80/20
Strawberries	40/10	170/40
Sugar	460/110	1840/440
Sultanas	290/70	1170/280
Sweetcorn - canned	80/20	330/80
Tagliatelle	40/105	1760/420
Tangerine - fresh	20/5	80/20
Tomatoes - raw	20/5	80/20
Tuna - no oil	290/70	1170/280
Turbot - raw	100/25	420/100
Turkey - no skin	125/30	500/120
Turnips	20/5	80/20
Veal - lean, no fat	125/30	500/120
Vegetable oils	1045/250	4200/1000
Whiting - raw	100/25	420/100
Winkles	20/5	60/15
Yeast		
fresh	60/15	250/60
dried	210/50	840/200
Yeast extract	210/50	840/200

SOUPS

Soup is not only an excellent starter but it can also make a satisfying snack meal for slimmers. Choose from the wide variety of soups featured here, from the sophisticated to the substantial. Refreshing iced soups are ideal for light summer lunches, served with a tangy salad; they also provide an elegant first course for a dinner party.

1 SPICED CARROT SOUP

Preparation time:
15 minutes

Cooking time:
25 minutes

Serves 4

Calories:
91 per portion

YOU WILL NEED:
1 onion, finely chopped
1 tablespoon olive oil
450 g/1 lb carrots, peeled and roughly chopped
1 slice fresh root ginger, 5 mm/ ¼ inch thick
generous pinch of mixed spice
1 teaspoon grated orange rind
600 ml/1 pint chicken stock
300 ml/½ pint skimmed milk
1 teaspoon chopped fresh coriander
FOR THE GARNISH
carrot slivers
fresh coriander sprigs

Fry the onion gently in the oil for 3 minutes; add the carrots and fry together for a further 2-3 minutes. Squeeze the fresh ginger in a garlic press and add the juice to the vegetables; add the mixed spice, orange rind, stock, skimmed milk and chopped coriander. Cover, bring to the boil and simmer gently for about 20 minutes, until the carrots are tender.

Blend the soup in a liquidizer until smooth. Reheat the soup, adjusting the consistency with a little extra stock if desired, then ladle into warmed soup bowls and garnish with the carrot slivers and coriander sprigs.

2 HERBY CHICKEN SOUP

Preparation time:
15 minutes

Cooking time:
10-15 minutes

Serves 4

Calories:
95 per portion

YOU WILL NEED:
2 teaspoons oil
1 onion, finely chopped
175 g/6 oz cooked chicken, chopped
900 ml/1½ pints boiling water
1 tablespoon soy sauce
small pinch of dried sage
small pinch of ground cinnamon
½ small garlic clove, crushed
2 tablespoons skimmed milk powder
2 tablespoons cold water
1 tablespoon chopped parsley
pepper

Heat the oil in a saucepan, add the onion and fry for 3 minutes, stirring, until transparent. Add the chicken, water, soy sauce, sage, cinnamon and garlic. Bring to the boil, then simmer for 5 minutes.

Combine the milk powder with the water. Stir a little of the soup into the milk, then slowly add this mixture to the pan, stirring constantly over a gentle heat. Add the parsley and pepper to taste.

■ COOK'S TIP

Fresh root ginger is available in most supermarkets. If you do not have a garlic press, use a pestle and mortar to extract the juice.

■ COOK'S TIP

Take care not to let the soup boil after the milk has been added or it may curdle. If you would like a slightly richer soup, use semi-skimmed fresh milk instead *of reconstituting the skimmed milk powder.*

3 PEPPER AND TOMATO SOUP

Preparation time:
20 minutes

Cooking time:
40 minutes

Serves 4

Calories:
58 per portion

YOU WILL NEED:
2 teaspoons vegetable oil
1 onion, finely chopped
2 green peppers, seeded and chopped
1 garlic clove, crushed
450 g/1 lb tomatoes, peeled and
  chopped
1 tablespoon tomato purée
750 ml/1¼ pints vegetable stock
1 teaspoon dried basil
salt and pepper
FOR THE GARNISH
2 tablespoons natural low-fat yogurt
fresh basil leaves

Heat the oil in a pan and fry the onion until soft. Add the green pepper and cook for 2 minutes. Stir in the garlic, tomatoes, tomato purée, stock, basil, salt and pepper. Bring to the boil, cover and simmer for 30 minutes. Allow to cool slightly. Put in a liquidizer or food processor and work to a purée.

Before serving, reheat and check the seasoning. Pour into warmed bowls and garnish with the yogurt and basil.

4 CARROT AND SAGE SOUP

Preparation time:
15 minutes

Cooking time:
50 minutes

Serves 6

Calories:
71 per portion

YOU WILL NEED:
25 g/1 oz butter
1 large onion, finely chopped
750 g/1 ½ lb carrots, finely sliced
1.75 litres/3 pints stock
salt and pepper
1 tablespoon chopped fresh sage
fresh sage sprigs, to garnish (optional)

Melt the butter in a large heavy-based pan and gently fry the onion until transparent, then add the carrots and stock. Season with salt and pepper. Bring to the boil and simmer, uncovered, for about 30 minutes.

Liquidize the soup, then return to the pan and add the chopped sage. Bring to the boil and simmer for another 15 minutes. Serve, garnished with sage sprigs, if using.

▊ COOK'S TIP

To remove the last scrap of purée from a tube of tomato purée remove the cap and slowly roll a rolling pin over the tube.

▊ COOK'S TIP

Fresh sage is usually available in large supermarkets during the winter months. If you cannot find any, dried sage may be used instead. Soak the leaves first in a tablespoon of warmed dry white wine for about 20 minutes.

5 JERUSALEM ARTICHOKE SOUP

Preparation time:
20 minutes

Cooking time:
35 minutes

Serves 4

Calories:
138 per portion

YOU WILL NEED:
500 g/1 ¼ lb Jerusalem artichokes,
  scraped clean
3 tablespoons lemon juice
1 tablespoon sunflower oil
900 ml/1 ½ pints marrowbone or
  chicken stock
1 teaspoon dried dill
½ teaspoon sugar
salt and pepper
FOR THE LEMON CROÛTONS
4 slices crustless bread
1 tablespoon lemon juice

Chop the artichokes into small pieces, sprinkling them liberally with lemon juice as you work to help prevent them discolouring.

Heat the oil and add the artichokes, stir well. Cover and sweat over a gentle heat for 1-2 minutes. Pour on the stock, bring to the boil, cover and simmer for about 30 minutes. Liquidize the artichokes, adding the dried dill and sugar, then rub through a sieve and return to the pan. Reheat, and add salt and pepper to taste.

To make the lemon croûtons, brush both sides of the slices of bread with lemon juice and toast until lightly coloured on both sides. Cut into cubes.

Serve the soup, garnished with the croûtons.

▌COOK'S TIP

Jerusalem artichokes are not related to globe artichokes – they are members of the sunflower family which is why sunflower oil is the best one to use.

6 CELERY AND ALMOND SOUP

Preparation time:
15 minutes

Cooking time:
15 minutes

Serves 4

Calories:
156 per portion

YOU WILL NEED:
1 small onion, finely chopped
6 celery sticks, finely chopped
1 tablespoon coarsely chopped parsley
1 teaspoon dill seed
50 g/2 oz blanched almonds
300 ml/½ pint chicken stock
300 ml/½ pint skimmed milk
3 tablespoons natural low-fat yogurt
1 egg yolk
1 tablespoon toasted flaked almonds,
  to garnish

Put the onion, celery, parsley, dill seed, almonds, stock and milk into a saucepan; bring to the boil and simmer gently for about 12 minutes until the vegetables are tender.

Blend the soup in a liquidizer until smooth. Return to a clean saucepan. Beat the yogurt with the egg yolk and stir into the soup. Reheat the soup gently; do not allow it to boil.

Ladle into small bowls and sprinkle with the toasted almonds.

▌COOK'S TIP

To toast the almonds, put them in a thick-based frying pan over a low heat for 2-3 minutes, stirring constantly. Do not use any fat as the oil in the nuts will be *sufficient to prevent them sticking to the pan.*

7 TOMATO AND WATERCRESS SOUP

Preparation time:
15 minutes

Cooking time:
30 minutes

Serves 4

Calories:
46 per portion

YOU WILL NEED:
450 g/1 lb tomatoes, peeled and
  chopped
2 tablespoons fine oatmeal
1 teaspoon paprika
1 teaspoon dried oregano
2 tablespoons chopped mint
2 bay leaves
1 blade of mace
6 peppercorns
4-6 parsley stalks
2 tablespoons celery leaves
750 ml/1¼ pints chicken stock
1 bunch watercress sprigs, trimmed
2 teaspoons lemon juice
salt and pepper
celery leaves, to garnish

Put the tomatoes into a saucepan over a moderate heat and stir in the oatmeal and paprika. When well blended, stir in the oregano and mint. Tie the bay leaves, mace, peppercorns, parsley and celery leaves in a piece of muslin and add with the stock. Stir well and bring the soup to the boil slowly, stirring constantly. Cover the pan and simmer for 20 minutes. Discard the bag of flavourings. Put the soup in a liquidizer and purée.

Return the purée to the pan. Chop the watercress, stir it into the purée with the lemon juice and season with salt and pepper. Simmer for about 3 minutes until the watercress is just tender. Garnish the soup with celery leaves and serve hot.

■ COOK'S TIP

A good home-made stock is the secret of delicious soups. It is well worth making a large quantity and freezing it in different sized containers.

8 MARROW AND DILL SOUP

Preparation time:
15 minutes, plus
standing time

Cooking time:
20 minutes

Serves 4

Calories:
83 per portion

YOU WILL NEED:
1 kg/2¼ lb marrow, peeled, seeded
  and grated
salt
1½ teaspoons oil
1½ teaspoons plain flour
1 tablespoon mild French mustard
1 tablespoon dried dill
900 ml/1½ pints chicken stock
1 tablespoon lemon juice
1 teaspoon sugar (optional)
paprika, to garnish

Put the marrow in a colander, sprinkle a little salt over and leave to stand for 20 minutes.

Heat the oil in a large saucepan, put in the marrow and sprinkle with the flour. Stir well, then cook for 1 minute, stirring all the time. Add the mustard and half the dill, stir, then pour the stock in slowly, still stirring. Cover and simmer very gently for 15-20 minutes, do not allow to boil vigorously.

For a smooth-textured soup, cool slightly, then blend in a liquidizer. Taste and adjust the seasoning, adding lemon juice and sugar as necessary. Stir in the remaining dill. Pour into warmed soup bowls, sprinkle a little paprika over each portion and serve.

■ COOK'S TIP

For a richer soup, put one teaspoonful of smetana in the bottom of each bowl before the soup is poured in. This will increase the calories per portion slightly.

9   GREEN GARDEN SOUP

Preparation time:
20 minutes

Cooking time:
30-35 minutes

Serves 4

Calories:
103 per portion

YOU WILL NEED:
4 celery sticks, chopped
2 leeks, cleaned and chopped
1 bunch watercress, washed and
    chopped
1 heart of a round lettuce, shredded
4 spring onions, chopped
1 tablespoon chopped fresh tarragon
1 garlic clove, crushed
1 small head fennel, shredded
600 ml/1 pint chicken stock
300 ml/½ pint skimmed milk
salt and pepper
50 g/2 oz fine green fettucine, broken
    into short lengths

Put the celery, leeks, watercress, lettuce, spring onions, tarragon, garlic and fennel into a large saucepan; add the stock, skimmed milk and salt and pepper to taste. Simmer the soup for 20-25 minutes until all the vegetables are tender.

Blend the soup in a liquidizer until smooth. Return the soup to a clean pan and bring to the boil; add the broken fettucine and simmer for about 4 minutes, until the pasta is just tender. Serve the soup piping hot.

10   TOMATO AND CARROT SOUP

Preparation time:
10 minutes

Cooking time:
35 minutes

Serves 4

Calories:
38 per portion

YOU WILL NEED:
1 x 400 g/14 oz can tomatoes,
    chopped
2 large carrots, grated
1 small onion, finely chopped
300 ml/½ pint stock
1 teaspoon oregano
grated nutmeg
salt
1 bay leaf
1 teaspoon brown sugar
1 tablespoon chopped parsley, to
    garnish

Put the tomatoes and their juice in a saucepan. Add the carrot, onion, stock, oregano, nutmeg and salt to taste, bay leaf and sugar. Bring to the boil, stirring, cover and simmer for 30 minutes. Remove the bay leaf.

Pour the soup into a warmed tureen and sprinkle with parsley.

■ COOK'S TIP

Cooked fennel has a milder and sweeter flavour than raw. It has a distinctive aniseed taste. It is available from autumn to spring.

■ COOK'S TIP

The teaspoonful of brown sugar brings out the flavour of the vegetables. Either chicken stock or, if you are a vegetarian, a stock made from root vegetables would *be suitable for this economical recipe.*

11 ONION AND WATERCRESS SOUP

Preparation time:
10 minutes

Cooking time:
25 minutes

Serves 4

Calories:
29 per portion

YOU WILL NEED:
1 bunch watercress
2 onions, sliced
900 ml/1½ pints light chicken stock
grated nutmeg
salt and pepper
40 g/1½ oz skimmed milk powder
few watercress leaves, to garnish

Wash the watercress, remove the coarse stalks and chop roughly. Put in a saucepan with the onion, stock and grated nutmeg, and salt and pepper to taste. Bring to the boil, cover and simmer for 20 minutes. Leave to cool slightly.

Put the watercress mixture in a liquidizer with the skimmed milk powder. Blend until smooth, then return to the pan. Bring to the boil, stirring, and cook for 1-2 minutes. Check the seasoning and pour into warmed bowls. Garnish with the watercress leaves.

◼ COOK'S TIP

Watercress is rich in vitamins and minerals. Its spicy, pungent flavour gives a piquancy to this soup. Discard any blemished or discoloured leaves.

12 PROVENCAL VEGETABLE SOUP

Preparation time:
30 minutes

Cooking time:
30 minutes

Serves 6

Calories:
291 per portion

YOU WILL NEED:
250 g/9 oz courgettes, chopped
100 g/4 oz leeks, chopped
450 g/1 lb tomatoes, peeled and chopped
175 g/6 oz carrots, chopped
450 g/1 lb onions, chopped
250 g/9 oz young runner beans
250 g/9 oz French beans
250 g/9 oz broad beans, shelled weight
1.2 litres/2 pints veal or chicken stock
salt and pepper
100 g/4 oz short-cut macaroni
50 g/2 oz Parmesan cheese, grated
FOR THE PESTO
3 garlic cloves
9 basil sprigs
3 tablespoons olive oil

Put the vegetables in a large saucepan. Add the veal or chicken stock, and season to taste with salt and pepper. Bring to the boil, cover and simmer for 15 minutes. Add the macaroni and cook for 10-12 minutes.

Meanwhile, make the pesto. Put the garlic and basil in a mortar and pound to a paste. Add the oil, drop by drop. Remove the soup from the heat and stir in the pesto.

Ladle into a warmed tureen or individual bowls, sprinkle with Parmesan cheese and serve immediately.

◼ COOK'S TIP

Fresh basil must be used for making the pesto. If it is unobtainable, omit the pesto and add 2 crushed garlic cloves and 1 tablespoon chopped parsley to the soup, with the stock. Alternatively, use 2-3 tablespoons prepared pesto sauce which is available in large supermarkets.

13 ADUKI BEAN SOUP

Preparation time:
15 minutes, plus soaking

Cooking time:
1¼ hours

Serves 4

Calories:
174 per portion

YOU WILL NEED:

100 g/4 oz aduki beans
2 tablespoons oil
1 onion, chopped
1 celery stick, chopped
1 carrot, chopped
1 garlic clove, crushed
2 tomatoes, peeled and chopped
1 tablespoon tomato purée
1 bay leaf
1 teaspoon chopped thyme
900 ml/1½ pints stock or water
salt and pepper
chopped parsley

Soak the beans in cold water to cover for 3 hours; drain well.

Heat the oil in a large saucepan, add the onion, celery and carrot and cook until softened. Add the remaining ingredients, with salt and pepper to taste. Bring to the boil, boil for 10 minutes, then simmer for 1 hour.

Pour into a warmed soup tureen and sprinkle with the parsley to serve.

14 FISH AND LEEK SOUP

Preparation time:
15 minutes

Cooking time:
20 minutes

Serves 4

Calories:
177 per portion

YOU WILL NEED:

1 small onion, thinly sliced
1 garlic clove, crushed
2 tablespoons olive oil
2 medium leeks, cleaned and cut into fine strips
2 tablespoons chopped parsley
225 g/8 oz white fish fillet, cubed
300 ml/½ pint chicken stock
300 ml/½ pint skimmed milk
salt and pepper
3 tablespoons natural low-fat yogurt
1 egg yolk
1 tablespoon finely chopped green pepper, to garnish

Fry the onion and garlic gently in the olive oil for 3 minutes; add the leeks and parsley and fry for a further 3 minutes. Add the cubed fish, stock, skimmed milk and salt and pepper to taste; bring to the boil and simmer gently for 10 minutes.

Beat the yogurt and egg yolk together. Blend with a little of the hot soup and then add to the remaining soup in the pan. Heat through gently, without boiling, for 1-2 minutes.

Serve piping hot, garnished with the finely chopped green pepper.

▧ COOK'S TIP

Aduki (or adzuki) beans have a sweet but fairly strong flavour. These tiny, dark red beans are rich in protein. If unobtainable, substitute kidney beans.

▧ COOK'S TIP

If you like a more pronounced taste of fish, replace the chicken stock with fish stock made from the skin and trimmings. This soup is substantial *enough to make a light meal on a winter's day.*

15   MUSSEL CHOWDER

Preparation time:
15 minutes

Cooking time:
30 minutes

Serves 4

Calories:
183 per portion

YOU WILL NEED:
1 green pepper, seeded and chopped
1 small onion, chopped
350 g/12 oz potatoes, chopped
1 litre/1¾ pints fish or chicken stock
1 x 425 g/15 oz can shelled mussels,
*   drained*
salt and pepper
4 tablespoons skimmed milk powder
chopped parsley, to garnish

Put the pepper, onion, potatoes and stock in a large saucepan and bring to the boil. Reduce the heat, skim off the scum that rises to the surface, cover and simmer for 20 minutes.

Add the mussels and season to taste with salt and pepper, then simmer for a further 5 minutes. Cool slightly. Stir in the milk powder. Serve hot, garnished with chopped parsley.

16   HEARTY FISH SOUP

Preparation time:
20 minutes

Cooking time:
15 minutes

Serves 4

Calories:
122 per portion

YOU WILL NEED:
1 x 175 g/6 oz portion haddock, fresh
*   or frozen and thawed*
1 x 175 g/6 oz portion cod, fresh or
*   frozen and thawed*
1 tablespoon oil
2 onions, thinly sliced
1 celery stick, finely chopped
2 garlic cloves, crushed
1 x 400 g/14 oz can chopped tomatoes
2 tablespoons peeled prawns
juice of ½ lemon
½ teaspoon sugar
1 tablespoon chopped parsley
3 pinches of ground bay leaves
pinch of dried thyme
generous pinch of powdered saffron
pepper to taste
600 ml/1 pint boiling water

Cut the fish into small pieces. Heat the oil in a saucepan, add the onion and fry for 2 minutes, without browning. Add the celery and fry for 2 minutes, stirring.

Stir in the remaining ingredients, bring to the boil, then cover and simmer for 8-10 minutes. Serve hot.

▌COOK'S TIP

To use fresh mussels, buy 1.5 kg/3 lb mussels in their shells. Scrub, pulling off the beards and discarding any open mussels. Cook quickly in stock for 5-6 minutes.

▌COOK'S TIP

Dried bay leaves keep their flavour for a long time, stored in a screw-topped jar. Crush 2-3 leaves in a pestle and mortar for this soup.

17 RASAN SOUP

Preparation time:
15 minutes, plus
soaking

Cooking time:
55 minutes

Serves 4

Calories:
120 per portion

YOU WILL NEED:
100 g/4 oz yellow split peas, soaked
overnight and drained
1 onion, finely chopped
2 celery sticks, thinly sliced
1 small leek, trimmed and thinly sliced
2 teaspoons grated lemon rind
3 tablespoons lemon juice
½ teaspoon ground turmeric
2 tablespoons medium oatmeal
1 litre/1¾ pints chicken stock
salt and pepper
4 tablespoons natural low-fat yogurt
(optional)
4 thin lemon slices, to garnish

Put the split peas, onion, celery, leek, lemon rind, lemon juice, turmeric and oatmeal into a saucepan, stir them together and pour on the stock. Bring to the boil, cover and simmer for 45 minutes. Season with salt and pepper and simmer for a further 5 minutes.

Swirl the yogurt on top, if using, and garnish the soup with the lemon slices. Serve hot.

18 AVGOLEMONO

Preparation time:
10 minutes

Cooking time:
25-30 minutes

Serves 4

Calories:
94 per portion

YOU WILL NEED:
1.2 litres/2 pints chicken stock
2 teaspoons finely grated lemon rind
1 sprig parsley
1 sprig thyme
50 g/2 oz long-grain rice
salt and pepper
2 eggs
2 tablespoons lemon juice
lemon slices, to garnish

Pour the stock into a saucepan, add the lemon rind and herbs. Bring to the boil, add the rice and a little seasoning. Reduce the heat and simmer for 20 minutes, or until the rice is tender.

Beat the eggs and lemon juice together in a bowl, whisk in a little hot, but not boiling, stock from the saucepan. Pour the egg mixture into the hot soup; simmer very gently, stirring constantly, until the soup thickens. Add any extra seasoning required, remove the sprigs of herbs and serve at once topped with lemon slices.

▓ COOK'S TIP

Turmeric not only gives a distinctive flavour to the soup but also adds colour. Buy all spices in small quantities and store them in a cool dark place.

▓ COOK'S TIP

After the egg mixture has been added to the hot soup, the liquid must not be allowed to boil as the eggs may curdle. If preferred, a double saucepan can be *used but this will increase the cooking time a little.*

19 BORTSCH

Preparation time:
20 minutes, plus
cooling

Cooking time:
1¼ hours

Serves 4

Calories:
91 per portion

YOU WILL NEED:
2 teaspoons oil
1 onion, chopped
2 celery sticks, chopped
350 g/12 oz beetroot, chopped
100 g/4 oz white cabbage, shredded
900 ml/1½ pints stock
1 tablespoon vinegar
salt and pepper
1 bay leaf
about 3 tablespoons water
150 ml/¼ pint natural low-fat yogurt

Heat the oil in a saucepan, add the onion and celery and fry until soft. Add the beetroot and cabbage, then stir in the stock, vinegar, salt and pepper to taste, and bay leaf. Bring to the boil, cover and simmer for 1 hour.

Leave to cool slightly, remove the bay leaf, then purée in a liquidizer or rub through a sieve. Return to the pan, adding just enough water to give a pouring consistency. Check the seasoning and reheat. Pour into warmed serving bowls and stir in a little yogurt. Serve immediately.

20 ICED CUCUMBER SOUP

Preparation time:
15 minutes, plus
chilling

Cooking time:
15-20 minutes

Serves 4

Calories:
203 per portion

YOU WILL NEED:
25 g/1 oz butter
1 cucumber, chopped
2 shallots, chopped
450 ml/¾ pint semi-skimmed milk
2 garlic cloves, crushed
1 bay leaf
salt and pepper
1 tablespoon chopped mint
1 tablespoon chopped chives
250 g/9 oz prawns
5 tablespoons natural low-fat yogurt
3 tablespoons smetana
FOR THE GARNISH
mint sprigs
cucumber slices
peeled prawns

Melt the butter in a saucepan, add the cucumber and shallots, cover and cook gently for 5 minutes, until softened but not brown.

Add the milk, garlic, bay leaf, and salt and pepper to taste, and simmer for 10 minutes. Remove the bay leaf. Pour the soup into a liquidizer or food processor and work until smooth. Pour into a soup tureen and stir in the herbs, prawns, yogurt and smetana. Chill for 2 hours.

Garnish with mint, cucumber slices and prawns to serve.

▌COOK'S TIP

If the beetroot leaves are young and tender, they can be used as a vegetable. Wash the leaves carefully and boil or steam for 10-15 minutes.

▌COOK'S TIP

Follow this quite rich soup with a low-calorie main course! Cooking the vegetables in butter makes the soup taste better than using any other fat or oil.

Smetana gives a smooth texture to this soup.

21 CHILLED PEA SOUP

Preparation time:
20 minutes, plus chilling

Cooking time:
20 minutes

Serves 4

Calories:
118 per portion

YOU WILL NEED:
350 g/12 oz fresh shelled peas
225 g/8 oz potatoes, chopped
1 onion, chopped
1 large mint sprig
finely grated rind of ½ lemon
2 tablespoons lemon juice
900 ml/1½ pints chicken stock
salt and pepper
1 tablespoon chopped fresh mint, to garnish

Put the peas in a large saucepan with the potatoes, onion, mint sprig, lemon rind and juice and stock. Season with salt and pepper. Simmer, covered, for 15-20 minutes, or until the peas are tender.

Purée in a liquidizer or rub through a sieve. Set aside to cool.

Adjust the seasoning to taste and chill for 2-3 hours. Serve chilled, sprinkled with the mint.

22 CORIANDER YOGURT SOUP

Preparation time:
10 minutes, plus chilling

Serves 4

Calories:
83 per portion

YOU WILL NEED:
300 ml/½ pint natural low-fat yogurt
150 ml/¼ pint tomato juice
300 ml/½ pint semi-skimmed milk
1 garlic clove, crushed
1 small cucumber, peeled and finely diced
2 tablespoons chopped fresh coriander
salt and pepper
coriander sprigs, to garnish

Put the yogurt and tomato juice in a bowl and mix together thoroughly. Stir in the milk, garlic, cucumber, most of the chopped coriander, and salt and pepper to taste. Chill for 2 hours.

Pour the soup into a tureen, and sprinkle with the remaining coriander. Garnish with coriander sprigs to serve.

■ COOK'S TIP

If necessary, use frozen petits pois. They will take less time to cook so add them to the other ingredients in the pan after 5-10 minutes.

■ COOK'S TIP

Coriander is one of the oldest herbs in cultivation, The seeds are often used in Eastern cooking. The leaves are mildly aromatic.

23 JELLIED GRAPEFRUIT AND CUCUMBER SOUP

Preparation time:
10 minutes, plus
chilling and setting

Cooking time:
10 minutes

Serves 4

Calories:
105 per portion

YOU WILL NEED:
25 g/1 oz powdered gelatine
1 litre/1 ¾ pints unsweetened
 grapefruit juice
salt and pepper
1 cucumber, peeled and grated
4 lemon slices, to garnish

Dissolve the gelatine in 3 tablespoons of the grapefruit juice over a pan of simmering water. Add the remaining grapefruit juice, season with salt and pepper and allow to cool.

As the grapefruit mixture begins to thicken, stir in the grated cucumber. Allow the mixture to set in the refrigerator for about 2 hours.

To serve, chop the jelly roughly with a sharp knife and spoon into individual glasses. Garnish with lemon slices.

24 GAZPACHO

Preparation time:
25 minutes, plus
chilling

Serves 4

Calories:
33 per portion

YOU WILL NEED:
450 g/1 lb tomatoes, peeled, seeded
 and chopped
1 green pepper, seeded and roughly
 chopped
1 red pepper, seeded and roughly
 chopped
1 small onion, roughly chopped
1 large garlic clove, chopped
about 450 ml/¾ pint chicken stock
salt and pepper
1 tablespoon lemon juice (optional)
FOR THE GARNISH
ice cubes
cucumber slices
1 tablespoon finely chopped red
 pepper

Put the tomatoes, peppers, onions, garlic and chicken stock into a liquidizer; blend until fairly smooth. Pour the blended soup into a bowl and season to taste, adding the lemon juice if necessary. Cover the soup and chill for at least 3 hours.

Ladle the chilled soup into soup bowls; add an ice cube to each one, and float cucumber slices sprinkled with a little chopped red pepper on top.

▥ COOK'S TIP

If you leave some skin on one end of the cucumber, it will be easier to hold while you are grating it. Alternatively, you could use a food processor or vary the *soup by including the cucumber skin.*

▥ COOK'S TIP

To peel tomatoes, put them in boiling water, leave for 6-10 seconds, then lift out. When cool, make a nick in the top of each tomato and peel off the skin.

STARTERS

This chapter contains a truly international selection of recipes, including some from France, Italy and the Middle East. Mostly quick and easy to prepare, many of these dishes can also be served as a light meal and some are suitable for packed lunches and picnics.

25 AVOCADO WITH RASPBERRY VINAIGRETTE

Preparation time:
15 minutes

Serves 4

Calories:
267 per portion

YOU WILL NEED:
2 avocados, halved and stoned
1 tablespoon lemon juice
100 g/4 oz raspberries
2 tablespoons olive oil
1 tablespoon wine vinegar
½ teaspoon clear honey
salt and pepper
fennel leaves, to garnish (optional)

Peel each avocado half and place cut side down on a serving plate. Slice through the avocados lengthways, then separate the slices slightly. Brush lightly with the lemon juice.

Press the raspberries through a nylon sieve to remove the seeds, then mix with the oil, vinegar, honey and salt and pepper to taste. Spoon a little around each avocado and serve immediately, garnished with fennel if liked.

26 GLOBE ARTICHOKES

Preparation time:
25 minutes, plus cooling

Cooking time:
25-40 minutes

Serves 4

Calories:
100 per portion

YOU WILL NEED:
4 globe artichokes
3 tablespoons light French dressing (see recipe 181)

Pull off the tough outer leaves from each artichoke and cut off the stalks. The artichokes should stand upright when cooked. The tops of the leaves can be trimmed with a pair of kitchen scissors but this is not essential.

Wash the artichokes in cold water, then put into a large pan of boiling salted water to cover and cook until tender. The cooking time varies considerably; small young artichokes need about 25 minutes while large mature artichokes can take 35-40 minutes.

Remove from the water and drain thoroughly. Cut away and discard the 'choke'; this consists of the central inner leaves with a hairy growth at the base. Allow the artichokes to become completely cold. Serve with the dressing.

■ COOK'S TIP

Choose the avocados carefully, avoiding any that are bruised. The discoloured parts are edible but spoil the appearance of the fruit. It is best to buy slightly under- *ripe avocados and leave them in a warm kitchen for 24 hours.*

■ COOK'S TIP

To test if an artichoke is ready lift it out of the water and pull off an outer leaf; it should come away easily and the inner base of the leaf should be tender.

27 LEEKS A LA GRECQUE

Preparation time:
10 minutes,
plus cooling

Cooking time:
25 minutes

Serves 4

Calories:
63 per portion

YOU WILL NEED:
350 g/12 oz leeks
juice of ½ lemon
1 tablespoon oil
1 tablespoon water
1 garlic clove, crushed
3 tomatoes, peeled and chopped
salt and pepper
chopped parsley, to garnish

Remove the outer leaves from the leeks and cut into 2.5 cm/1 inch lengths. Wash thoroughly. Place in a pan with the remaining ingredients, adding salt and pepper to taste.

Heat gently to simmering point, then simmer for 20 minutes. Leave to cool in the liquid for about 45 minutes, then arrange in a serving dish and garnish with parsley.

28 MELON AND ANCHOVY SALAD

Preparation time:
15 minutes, plus
chilling

Serves 4

Calories:
61 per portion

YOU WILL NEED:
1 medium melon
1 x 50 g/2 oz can anchovy fillets
juice of 1 lemon
juice of 1 orange
watercress sprigs, to garnish

Halve the melon and discard the seeds. Scoop the flesh into a serving dish, using a melon baller. Alternatively, cut into small cubes.

Drain the anchovy fillets, reserving 1 tablespoon of the oil. Cut the anchovies into short slivers and add to the melon.

Mix the lemon and orange juice with the reserved anchovy oil and pour over the salad. Chill for about an hour before serving, garnished with watercress sprigs.

■ COOK'S TIP

Many people still think of leeks as a vegetable to be served hot in the winter. Young leeks are delicious served as a cold starter. You can use the outer leaves, well washed, to give extra flavour to a vegetable stock.

■ COOK'S TIP

Check that the melon is ripe by pressing the stalk end lightly; it should give a little. A ripe melon also has a distinctive scent.

29 MELON, TOMATO AND GRAPE VINAIGRETTE

Preparation time:
20 minutes

Serves 4

Calories:
169 per portion

YOU WILL NEED:
2 small Ogen melons
4 tomatoes, peeled, quartered and
    seeded
175 g/6 oz black grapes, halved and
    seeded
1 tablespoon sesame seeds, roasted
4 mint sprigs, to garnish
FOR THE DRESSING
2 teaspoons clear honey
5 teaspoons cider vinegar
4 teaspoons oil
1 teaspoon chopped mint
salt and pepper

To make the dressing, put all the ingredients in a screw-topped jar and shake well.

Cut the melons in half and discard the seeds. Scoop the flesh into balls, using a melon baller, or cut into cubes; reserve the shells. Place the melon in a bowl with the tomatoes and grapes. Pour over the dressing.

Toss well, then spoon the mixture into the melon shells. Sprinkle with sesame seeds and garnish with the mint sprigs.

30 MINTED MELON BASKET

Preparation time:
15 minutes, plus
chilling

Serves 4

Calories:
85 per portion

YOU WILL NEED:
2 small round melons
75 g/3 oz strawberries or raspberries
a few cucumber slices
2 teaspoons chopped mint
1-2 tablespoons fresh orange juice
FOR THE GARNISH
mint leaves
grated orange rind
finely chopped pistachio nuts or
    toasted almonds

Halve the melons and discard the seeds. Scoop the flesh into a bowl, using a melon baller. Mix with the strawberries or raspberries and add a few cucumber slices and the chopped mint. Moisten with the orange juice and spoon the mixture back into the melon shells. Chill for 2 hours.

Top with mint leaves and a sprinkling of grated orange rind, finely chopped pistachio nuts or toasted almonds.

▓ COOK'S TIP

To roast sesame seeds, sprinkle them over a baking sheet and cook in a moderate oven (180°C, 350°F, gas 4) for 15 minutes, stirring often.

▓ COOK'S TIP

The amount of orange juice depends on how juicy the melons are. When soft fruit is out of season, use skinless segments of orange instead of the strawberries or raspberries. The mixture will just take longer to prepare!

31 PEARS WITH CURD CHEESE

Preparation time:
15 minutes, plus
chilling

Serves 4

Calories:
151 per portion

YOU WILL NEED:
50 g/2 oz Stilton cheese
150 ml/¼ pint natural low-fat yogurt
100 g/4 oz curd cheese
salt and pepper
2 ripe dessert pears
FOR THE GARNISH
shredded lettuce leaves
1 tablespoon chopped chives

Mash the Stilton cheese with 1 tablespoon of the yogurt and set aside.

Place the curd cheese in a bowl and beat in the remaining yogurt, and salt and pepper to taste.

Peel, halve and core the pears. Divide the Stilton filling between each cavity.

Arrange the lettuce on a serving dish and place the pears, cut side down, on top. Spoon over the yogurt and curd cheese mixture and sprinkle with the chives. Serve the pears chilled.

32 HAZELNUT AND VEGETABLE ROLL

Preparation time:
20 minutes, plus
chilling

Serves 4

Calories:
256 per portion

YOU WILL NEED:
225 g/8 oz low-fat soft cheese
75 g/3 oz toasted hazelnuts, chopped
2 celery sticks, finely chopped
1 small green pepper, seeded and finely chopped
2 spring onions, finely chopped
1 carrot, finely grated
3 tablespoons chopped parsley
salt
pinch of cayenne pepper
radicchio or endive leaves
2 large tomatoes, thinly sliced
FOR THE COATING
3 tablespoons chopped fresh parsley
2 tablespoons toasted hazelnuts, chopped
2 tablespoons medium oatmeal

Mix together the cheese, nuts, celery, green pepper, onion, carrot and 3 tablespoons parsley. Season with salt and cayenne pepper. Beat the mixture well and shape it into a roll about 7.5 cm/3 inches in diameter. Wrap the roll in foil and chill it for 2-3 hours.

Make the coating. Mix together the parsley, nuts and oatmeal. Roll the cheese mixture in the coating until it is evenly covered. Line a serving dish with the salad leaves. Place the roll on them and garnish it with the tomato slices.

■ COOK'S TIP

Chives can be grown successfully in a flower pot on a sunny window-sill. The easiest way to chop them is to use a pair of sharp scissors.

■ COOK'S TIP

To serve this roll for lunch, prepare it the previous day and chill it overnight. You will then only have to roll the cheese mixture in the coating before serving it.

33   AVOCADO SALAD

Preparation time:
15 minutes

Serves 4

Calories:
372 per portion

YOU WILL NEED:
4 *large lettuce leaves*
3 *tablespoons oil*
4 *teaspoons white wine vinegar or*
   lemon juice
salt and pepper
2 *avocados*
4 *tomatoes, peeled and sliced*
75 *g/3 oz curd cheese*
1 *teaspoon finely chopped fresh*
   marjoram

Arrange the lettuce on four individual serving plates. Blend the oil, vinegar or lemon juice and a little seasoning together.

Halve the avocados, peel and remove the stones. Place on the lettuce leaves, cut side down; slice carefully. Arrange the tomato and cheese slices on the lettuce. Top with the dressing and the marjoram. Serve immediately.

34   TANGY GRAPEFRUIT

Preparation time:
15 minutes, plus chilling

Serves 4

Calories:
25 per portion

YOU WILL NEED:
2 *large grapefruit, halved*
½ *green pepper, seeded and chopped*
1 *carrot, grated*
2.5 *cm/1 inch piece of cucumber, diced*
freshly ground black pepper

Loosen the grapefruit from the skin and remove, leaving the empty half grapefruit shells intact. Scallop the edges of the shells, if wished.

Remove the pith and discard. Chop the fruit and place in a bowl with the juice. Add the remaining ingredients, with pepper to taste, and mix well. Cover the bowl with cling film and chill for at least 1 hour.

Just before serving, pile the mixture into the prepared grapefruit shells.

■ COOK'S TIP

If fresh marjoram is not available, replace with ½ teaspoonful of dried oregano. The inclusion of curd cheese in this recipe adds protein, making it a *good choice for a light meal as well as a starter.*

■ COOK'S TIP

If the grapefruit shells tend to roll around in the dish, carefully remove a thin slice from the base of each half with a sharp knife before filling them.

35 BURGHUL TOMATO CASES

Preparation time:
25 minutes, plus
soaking and
standing

Serves 4

Calories:
149 per portion

YOU WILL NEED:
50 g/2 oz fine cracked wheat (burghul)
¼ teaspoon salt
2 tablespoons lemon juice
8 large tomatoes
2 spring onions, finely chopped
8 tablespoons chopped fresh coriander
    or parsley
2 tablespoons chopped fresh mint
2 tablespoons olive oil
freshly ground black pepper
FOR THE GARNISH
salad leaves or vine leaves
mint sprigs
thin slices of lemon

Soak the cracked wheat in water for 15 minutes. Drain it, tip it into a clean tea towel and wring tightly to remove the excess moisture. Turn the cracked wheat into a bowl, sprinkle with salt and lemon juice and set aside for 1 hour.

Cut the tops from the tomatoes. Using a teaspoon or vegetable baller, scoop out the flesh and seeds and chop. Dry the tomato cases with absorbent kitchen paper. Stir the chopped tomato, spring onion, herbs and oil into the cracked wheat and season it with pepper.

Spoon the salad into the tomato cases. Place the tomato cases on a serving dish lined with salad leaves or vine leaves and garnish with mint springs and lemon.

36 SUNSHINE FRUIT KEBABS

Preparation time:
15 minutes, plus
marinating

Cooking time:
6-7 minutes

Serves 4

Calories:
173 per portion

YOU WILL NEED:
2 oranges
2 small grapefruit, peeled and
    segmented
8 pre-soaked prunes, stoned
4 tablespoons vegetable oil
1 tablespoon red wine vinegar
freshly ground black pepper
2 tablespoons chopped fresh mint
8 bay leaves

Peel and segment 1 orange. Cut the other orange in half lengthways. Peel and segment one half. Squeeze the juice and grate the rind from the other half. Thread the orange and grapefruit segments and the prunes on to four skewers. Place them on a flat dish.

Mix together the orange juice, orange rind, oil and vinegar, season with pepper and stir in the mint. Pour the dressing over the kebabs and turn them to coat them thoroughly. Set the kebabs aside for at least 1 hour, turning them occasionally if possible.

Place the kebabs under a preheated moderate grill and cook for 6-7 minutes, turning frequently until the fruit is brown. Thread a bay leaf at both ends of each skewer. Serve hot.

▌ COOK'S TIP

*If necessary, cut a very thin
slice from the base of each
tomato so that they stand
evenly on the serving dish.
Choose tomatoes that are
ripe but still quite firm.*

▌ COOK'S TIP

*Kebabs can also be cooked
on a barbecue. These fruit
kebabs are also perfect for
any vegetarian guests. Turn
the kebabs so that they
brown evenly.*

37 STUFFED MUSSELS

Preparation time:
20 minutes

Cooking time:
12-14 minutes

Oven temperature:
200°C, 400°F, gas 6

Serves 4

Calories:
175 per portion

YOU WILL NEED:
48 fresh mussels, scrubbed clean
salt
2 lemon slices
2 teaspoons lemon juice
50 g/2 oz soft margarine
1 tablespoon olive oil
3 garlic cloves, crushed
1 shallot, finely chopped
2 tablespoons chopped parsley
3 tablespoons fresh wholemeal
  breadcrumbs
FOR THE GARNISH
parsley sprigs
lemon wedges

Put the mussels in a pan of boiling salted water, add the lemon slices, cover and cook for about 7 minutes, until the mussels have opened. Remove with a slotted spoon, discarding any that have not opened. Remove the empty top shells from the mussels and discard.

Beat the remaining ingredients together and spread the mixture on top of the mussels. Place on a baking sheet and cook in the oven for 5 minutes or until golden.

Arrange on a warmed serving dish and garnish with the parsley and lemon.

38 SCALLOPS WITH DILL AND LIME

Preparation time:
10 minutes, plus
chilling

Cooking time:
5 minutes

Serves 4

Calories:
85 per portion

YOU WILL NEED:
juice of 2 limes
350 g/12 oz queens or scallops
salt and pepper
2 tablespoons chopped dill
1 tablespoon chopped mint
¼ cucumber, diced
2 teaspoons sunflower oil
FOR THE GARNISH
lime slices
mint sprigs

Pour the lime juice into a saucepan, add the queens or scallops, and salt and pepper to taste. Bring to the boil, then simmer for 2-3 minutes, until the shellfish turn white.

Remove from the heat and allow to cool. Add the dill, mint, cucumber and oil and place in a serving dish. Chill for 2 hours to allow the flavours to develop.

Garnish with lime slices and mint sprigs.

■ COOK'S TIP

Maybe because mussels are among the least expensive varieties of shellfish, they tend not to be fully appreciated in the British Isles. If you feel daunted by the amount of preparation needed, buy ready-cleaned mussels which only need rinsing and the beards pulling off.

■ COOK'S TIP

Queens are smaller than scallops and are ideal for starter dishes. Scallops, like oysters, are best when there is an 'R' in the month.

39 CHEESE AND FRUIT COCKTAIL

Preparation time:
20 minutes, plus chilling

Serves 4

Calories:
95 per portion

YOU WILL NEED:
2 dessert apples
lemon juice
2 celery sticks, chopped
50 g/2 oz Edam cheese, diced
100 g/4 oz grapes, halved and seeded
½ lettuce, shredded
grated rind and juice of 1 orange
2 tablespoons natural low-fat yogurt

Chop the apples and put in a bowl and sprinkle with lemon juice. Add the celery, cheese and grapes and mix together. Arrange a little shredded lettuce in the base of four dishes. Pile the cheese and fruit mixture on top.

Mix the orange rind, juice and yogurt together, then pour a little over each cocktail. Serve chilled.

40 CHEESE SLAW

Preparation time:
20 minutes

Serves 4

Calories:
275 per portion

YOU WILL NEED:
250 g/9 oz white cabbage, finely shredded
1 celery stick, chopped
2 carrots, grated
25 g/1 oz raisins
1 dessert apple
2 teaspoons lemon juice
175 g/6 oz Gouda cheese, coarsely grated
150 ml/¼ pint natural low-fat yogurt
salt and pepper
chopped parsley, to garnish

Place the cabbage, celery, carrot and raisins in a large bowl. Grate the apple and toss in the lemon juice. Add to the bowl with the cheese and mix well.

Season the yogurt with salt and pepper to taste, then stir into the salad. Pile on to a serving dish and garnish with chopped parsley.

■ COOK'S TIP

Always wash fresh fruit thoroughly in cold water. This is particularly necessary when using unpeeled fruit such as apples and grapes. A crisp variety of dessert apple will give a pleasant contrasting texture to the cheese.

■ COOK'S TIP

The easiest way to prepare the white cabbage is to cut it into thin slices with a serrated bread knife, then chop the shreds to a suitable size.

41 HADDOCK AND EGG MOUSSE

Preparation time:
15 minutes, plus setting

Cooking time:
10 minutes

Serves 4

Calories:
109 per portion

YOU WILL NEED:
175 g/6 oz smoked haddock
1 hard-boiled egg, chopped
200 ml/7 fl oz natural low-fat yogurt
1 teaspoon powdered gelatine
1 tablespoon water
1 teaspoon lemon juice
salt and pepper
FOR THE GARNISH
watercress sprigs
hard-boiled egg slices

Poach the haddock in a little water for 6 minutes. Drain, skin and flake the fish. Mix with the egg and yogurt.

Dissolve the gelatine in the lemon juice and water in a small bowl over a pan of simmering water. Cool and fold into the fish mixture with salt and pepper to taste. Spoon into four ramekin dishes and chill for about 2 hours, until set. Garnish with watercress and egg.

42 CRUNCHY STUFFED PEARS

Preparation time:
10 minutes

Serves 4

Calories:
117 per portion

YOU WILL NEED:
2 dessert pears
lemon juice
100 g/4 oz cottage cheese
25 g/1 oz walnuts, chopped
25 g/1 oz raisins
½ red dessert apple, grated
Worcestershire sauce
salt and pepper
lettuce and tomato, to garnish

Cut the pears in half, remove the core and sprinkle with lemon juice. Place the remaining ingredients in a bowl, adding Worcestershire sauce, salt and pepper to taste; mix well.

Pile the mixture into the pear halves, place each one on a lettuce leaf and garnish with lettuce and tomato.

■ COOK'S TIP

If you omit the garnish, you can cover the ramekins with cling film and include them in a picnic basket. They are equally useful as part of a packed lunch.

■ COOK'S TIP

If you do not like the taste of their skin, eat these pears with a teaspoon, like a halved avocado. The filling is a delicious contrast with the fruit.

43 PIPERADE

Preparation time:
15 minutes

Cooking time:
15-20 minutes

Serves 4

Calories:
384 per portion

YOU WILL NEED:
1 tablespoon olive oil
1 large onion, sliced
4 green peppers, seeded and sliced
750 g/1½ lb tomatoes, peeled and
  chopped
1 garlic clove, crushed
salt and pepper
1 tablespoon chopped basil
4 small gammon rashers, trimmed
4 eggs, beaten

Heat the oil in a frying pan. Add the onion and fry gently until soft. Add the peppers, tomatoes, garlic, and salt and pepper to taste. Cook until the tomatoes are pulpy. Add the basil.

Meanwhile, cook the gammon under a preheated moderate grill until tender, turning once. Place on a warmed serving dish and keep warm.

Add the eggs to the frying pan and stir until just scrambled. Remove from the heat and pile on top of the gammon. Serve immediately.

44 TURKISH AUBERGINES

Preparation time:
10 minutes

Cooking time:
25-30 minutes

Oven temperature:
200°C, 400°F, gas 6

Serves 4

Calories:
94 per portion

YOU WILL NEED:
2 aubergines
salt
ground mace
2 teaspoons olive oil
shredded rind of 1 orange, to garnish
FOR THE DRESSING
300 ml/½ pint natural low-fat yogurt
2 teaspoons olive oil
2 teaspoons fresh orange juice
pinch of ground mace
salt and pepper

Halve the aubergines lengthways and sprinkle with a little salt and mace.

Cut four pieces of foil each large enough to contain an aubergine half. Lightly brush each aubergine half with oil and wrap in the foil. Bake for 25-30 minutes, or until tender.

Meanwhile, to make the dressing, mix together the yogurt, olive oil, orange juice, mace and salt and pepper.

Unwrap the aubergines and place on a serving dish. Pour the dressing over the hot aubergine halves, sprinkle with orange rind and serve immediately.

■ COOK'S TIP

As gammon tends to be rather salty, use the minimum of salt to season the vegetable mixture. Choose a light main course to follow this substantial starter or perhaps just a fruit dessert.

■ COOK'S TIP

For a sharper-tasting dressing, substitute lemon juice for the orange juice. Use finely chopped mint instead of orange rind as a garnish.

45   ZUCCHINI AL FORNO

Preparation time:
15 minutes, plus
cooling

Cooking time:
55 minutes

Oven temperature:
200°C, 400°F, gas 6

Serves 4

Calories:
61 per portion

YOU WILL NEED:
5 large or 10 small courgettes,
   trimmed
salt and pepper
1 teaspoon oil
1 garlic clove, finely chopped
1 x 500 g/1¼ lb can tomatoes
1 x 50 g/2 oz can anchovies, drained
1 teaspoon chopped marjoram (fresh
   or dried)

Slice the courgettes in half lengthways, and scoop out the seeds and pulp with a teaspoon. Sprinkle the inside of each courgette with salt and leave to drain upside down on absorbent kitchen paper.

Heat the oil in a saucepan and lightly fry the garlic. Rub the tomatoes through a sieve to remove the seeds and add the pulp to the pan. Bring to the boil and cook vigorously until reduced by half. Remove from the heat and stir in one chopped anchovy fillet and half the marjoram.

Wipe the insides of the courgettes with absorbent kitchen paper to remove the salt and set them in a large baking dish; fill each one with the tomato sauce and arrange anchovy fillets on top. Grind over plenty of black pepper and bake for about 40 minutes. Allow to cool before serving, sprinkled with the remaining marjoram.

46   OEUFS EN GELEE A L'ESTRAGON

Preparation time:
15 minutes, plus
infusing and chilling

Cooking time:
8-9 minutes

Serves 4

Calories:
120 per portion

YOU WILL NEED:
4 eggs
1 x 400 g/14 oz can consommé
6 tarragon sprigs
2 slices Parma ham, trimmed and
   halved
4 tarragon leaves, to garnish

Boil the eggs for 5-6 minutes. Remove from the saucepan, cool in cold water, then shell carefully.

Put the consommé in a saucepan with the tarragon sprigs; heat gently to simmering point. Remove from the heat and leave to infuse for 15 minutes, then discard the tarragon.

Wrap a piece of ham around each egg. Place the eggs in individual ramekin dishes. Spoon over the consommé and float a tarragon leaf on top. Chill until set.

■ COOK'S TIP

This Italian way of cooking courgettes is great for entertaining. It can be prepared in advance, covered with cling film and kept in the refrigerator until *needed. Sprinkle with marjoram at the last moment.*

■ COOK'S TIP

A good quality brand of canned consommé makes a very acceptable substitute for home-made consommé. Fresh tarragon is available in supermarkets.

47 FLAGEOLETS VINAIGRETTE

Preparation time:
20 minutes, plus
soaking overnight
and cooling

Cooking time:
1 hour 10 minutes

Serves 4

Calories:
285 per portion

YOU WILL NEED:
250 g/9 oz flageolet beans, soaked
overnight
salt
3 tablespoons light French dressing
(see Recipe 181)
1 red pepper, seeded and chopped
4 spring onions, chopped
1 tablespoon chopped mixed herbs
2 celery sticks, sliced

Drain the beans, place in a pan and cover with cold water. Bring to the boil and boil rapidly for 10 minutes. Cover and simmer for about 1 hour until tender, adding a little salt towards the end of the cooking. Drain thoroughly and place in a bowl.

Pour over the dressing while still warm and mix well. Leave to cool, then add the remaining ingredients. Toss thoroughly and transfer to a shallow dish to serve.

48 DUTCH AVOCADO

Preparation time:
20 minutes

Serves 2

Calories:
299 per portion

YOU WILL NEED:
1 small avocado
2 tablespoons lemon juice
1 eating apple
25 g/1 oz sultanas
1 teaspoon mild curry powder
2 tablespoons natural low-fat yogurt
salt and pepper

Halve the avocado and remove the stone. Score the flesh into small squares with a sharp pointed knife, cutting through almost to the skin. Scoop the flesh into a bowl and sprinkle with 1½ teaspoons of the lemon juice.

Peel and core the apple and cut into cubes the same size as the avocado. Soak the sultanas in the remaining lemon juice for 5 minutes. Combine the avocado, apple and sultanas.

Mix the curry powder with the yogurt and combine with the avocado mixture. Season with salt and pepper and pile into the avocado skins. Serve immediately.

■ COOK'S TIP

Pulses such as flageolet beans should play an important part in a calorie-controlled diet. They are a rich source of fibre which provides roughage.

■ COOK'S TIP

If you want to prepare the avocado in advance, cover each filled half tightly with cling film and put in the refrigerator to chill. The lemon juice will help to *prevent the avocado flesh from discolouring.*

FISH

Many of us grew up with the impression that fish meant fish and chips, with limp white fish deep-fried in greasy batter. Choose instead from the vast selection of fish and seafood which is readily available today. This chapter shows some imaginative ways of preparing this very nutritious, high-protein food. Some of the recipes are primarily for entertaining while others make economical family meals.

49 PLAICE WITH CUCUMBER

Preparation time: 15 minutes	YOU WILL NEED: 4 plaice fillets, about 65 g/2 ½ oz each
Cooking time: 5 minutes	25 g/1 oz margarine, melted pepper 1 tablespoon oil
Serves 4	2 spring onions, chopped, including green part
Calories: 152 per portion	50 g/2 oz mushrooms, thinly sliced ½ cucumber, quartered lengthways, then thinly sliced juice of 1 lemon lemon wedges, to garnish

Lay the fish in a lightly oiled grill pan, brush with the melted margarine and season with pepper. Cook under a preheated moderate grill for 3-4 minutes, turning the fish once.

Heat the oil in a frying pan, add the spring onions and fry for 30 seconds, stirring, without browning. Add the mushrooms and stir-fry for 1 minute. Add the cucumber and lemon juice and heat through.

Arrange the fish on warmed serving plates and garnish with the lemon wedges. Serve with the mushroom mixture and grilled tomatoes.

50 HADDOCK AND SPINACH LAYER

Preparation time: 15 minutes	YOU WILL NEED: 500 g/1¼ lb haddock fillets
Cooking time: 35-40 minutes	150 ml/¼ pint skimmed milk 1 bay leaf salt and pepper
Oven temperature: 180°C, 350°F, gas 4	1 hard-boiled egg, chopped 500 g/1¼ lb frozen leaf spinach
Serves 4	2 crispbreads, crushed 1 tomato, sliced, to garnish
Calories: 281 per portion	FOR THE SAUCE about 150 ml/¼ pint skimmed milk 25 g/1 oz margarine 1 onion, chopped 25 g/1oz plain flour grated nutmeg

Place the haddock in a pan. Add the milk, bay leaf, salt and pepper to taste, then poach for about 10 minutes until the fish is tender. Drain, reserving the liquor. Flake the haddock and mix with the egg. Cook the spinach and drain.

Make the fish liquor up to 300 ml/½ pint with extra milk. Melt the margarine in a pan and fry the onion until soft. Stir in the flour and cook for 1 minute. Gradually blend in the milk, then bring to the boil, stirring continuously. Cook, stirring, for a further 1 minute. Stir in the fish mixture; mix well. Layer the spinach and fish mixture in a greased 1.2 litre/2 pint ovenproof dish, finishing with the spinach. Sprinkle with the crispbreads and cook in the oven for 20-25 minutes. Garnish with the sliced tomato.

■ COOK'S TIP

If possible, buy whole plaice and do the filleting yourself. It will take a little time but you will have the trimmings to make stock and your fish will stay fresher as it loses some of its flavour when skinned and filleted.

■ COOK'S TIP

Crush the crispbreads quite finely so they will sprinkle easily over the spinach. Cover the crispbreads with greaseproof paper and press gently with a rolling pin.

51 HADDOCK WITH GRAPEFRUIT AND MUSHROOMS

Preparation time:
20 minutes

Cooking time:
30 minutes

Oven temperature:
180°C, 350°F, gas 4

Serves 4

Calories:
226 per portion

YOU WILL NEED:
4 haddock fillets, skinned, about
   175 g/6 oz each
40 g/1½ oz butter or margarine
3 spring onions, chopped
salt and pepper
2 grapefruit
100 g/4 oz mushrooms, sliced

Arrange the haddock fillets in a lightly greased casserole. Mash the butter or margarine with the spring onions and salt and pepper to taste. Grate the rind from the grapefruit and beat into the butter or margarine. Spread this over the haddock fillets. Cover with the mushrooms.

Squeeze the juice from one grapefruit and peel and segment the other. Pour the grapefruit juice over the mushrooms and place the grapefruit segments on top.

Cover and cook in the oven for about 30 minutes, or until the fish is cooked.

52 SKATE WITH COURGETTES

Preparation time:
20 minutes

Cooking time:
20-25 minutes

Oven temperature:
200°C, 400°F, gas 6

Serves 4

Calories:
400 per portion

YOU WILL NEED:
1 ½ teaspoons oil
4 skate wings, rinsed
1-2 tablespoons lemon juice
salt and pepper
lemon slices, to garnish
FOR THE TOPPING
4 courgettes, trimmed
2 tablespoons oil
1 onion, thinly sliced
1 x 50 g/2 oz can anchovy fillets,
   drained and chopped
1 tablespoon capers

Put a large sheet of foil on a flat baking sheet. Brush with half the oil. Lay the skate wings side by side on the foil. Sprinkle with the lemon juice and season to taste. Brush a second sheet of foil with the remaining oil and lay over the fish. Press the edges of the two sheets of foil together. Bake in the oven for 20-25 minutes.

Meanwhile, to make the topping, cut the unpeeled courgettes into thick matchstick pieces. Heat the oil in a frying pan, cook the onion until soft, then add the courgettes and continue cooking for 5 minutes. Turn the courgettes once or twice; they should retain a fairly firm texture when cooked. Add the anchovies, capers and a little pepper and heat for 1-2 minutes.

Arrange the skate on a warmed dish, pour any juices left from baking over the fish, then spoon the courgette mixture on top. Garnish with the lemon slices.

■ COOK'S TIP

To peel the grapefruit, remove the skin in sections, cutting deeply enough to remove the pith. Using the tip of the knife, ease out the skinless segments.

■ COOK'S TIP

The skate will feel sticky because of its gelatinous nature which makes it easy to bone. Rinse well in cold water before cooking. The raw fish smells slightly of *ammonia which will disappear when cooked.*

53 STIR-FRIED FISH

Preparation time:	YOU WILL NEED:
15 minutes, plus standing	500 g/1¼ lb cod fillet, skinned
	1 teaspoon salt
Cooking time:	1 tablespoon oil
5 minutes	2 rindless rashers back bacon, shredded
Serves 4	50 g/2 oz frozen peas, cooked
	50 g/2 oz frozen sweetcorn, cooked
Calories:	6 tablespoons chicken stock or water
192 per portion	2 teaspoons dry sherry
	2 teaspoons soy sauce
	1 teaspoon sugar
	1 teaspoon cornflour, blended with 1 teaspoon water
	spring onion flowers, to garnish (see Recipe 96)

Cut the cod fillet into 2.5 cm/1 inch wide strips, sprinkle with salt, leave for 15 minutes.

Heat the oil in a frying pan, add the fish and bacon and stir-fry for 3 minutes. Add the remaining ingredients, except the blended cornflour, and bring to the boil. Stir in the blended cornflour and cook for 1 minute.

Garnish the finished dish with the spring onion flowers and serve immediately.

54 FISH CASSEROLE WITH PEPPERS

Preparation time:	YOU WILL NEED:
15 minutes	1 tablespoon oil
	3 spring onions, chopped, including green part
Cooking time:	1 green pepper, seeded and cut into strips
25-30 minutes	
Oven temperature:	1 red pepper, seeded and cut into strips
180°C, 350°F, gas 4	
Serves 4-6	1 x 400 g/14 oz can chopped tomatoes
Calories:	½ teaspoon sugar
135 per portion	4-6 frozen cod fillets, thawed
	juice of 1 lemon
	pepper
	1 tablespoon chopped parsley

Heat the oil in a flameproof casserole, add the spring onions and fry for about 1 minute, stirring, without browning. Add the peppers and stir-fry for about 3 minutes.

Add the tomatoes, with their juice, and sugar and bring to the boil. Simmer for 5 minutes, then lay the cod on top. Squeeze over the lemon juice, season with pepper and sprinkle with the parsley. Cover and cook in the oven for 15-20 minutes, depending on the thickness of the fillets.

Serve each portion of fish with some of the pepper mixture.

■ COOK'S TIP

Stir-frying requires less fat or oil than other types of frying. It also reduces the cooking time to the minimum. The food retains colour and texture.

■ COOK'S TIP

Canned chopped tomatoes do cost a little more than the ordinary plum tomatoes. They not only save time but also seem to taste better. Avoid the varieties with

herbs if you are adding them to a dish with a well-defined flavour.

55 COD STEAKS RIVIERA

Preparation time:
15 minutes

Cooking time:
30 minutes

Serves 4

Calories:
199 per portion

YOU WILL NEED:
1 large onion, sliced into rings
1 garlic clove, crushed
350 g/12 oz tomatoes, peeled and sliced
1 tablespoon tomato purée
1 green pepper, seeded and sliced into rings
2 bay leaves
salt and pepper
4 cod steaks, about 175 g/6 oz each
1 tablespoon lemon juice
50 g/2 oz stuffed olives, halved
1 tablespoon chopped parsley
FOR THE GARNISH
25 g/1 oz hazelnuts, chopped
lemon twists
parsley sprigs

Put the onion, garlic, tomatoes, tomato purée, green pepper rings and bay leaves into a frying pan. Season with salt and pepper, stir well, bring to the boil, cover and simmer over a low heat for 10 minutes. Place the fish steaks on the vegetables, sprinkle on the lemon juice and cover the pan. Simmer for 12-15 minutes, or until the fish is just cooked.

Stir in the olives and parsley and just heat through. Using a fish slice, transfer the fish and vegetable sauce to a warmed serving dish. Discard the bay leaves. Sprinkle on the hazelnuts and garnish with the lemon twists and parsley sprigs.

56 KEDGEREE

Preparation time:
15 minutes

Cooking time:
25 minutes

Serves 4

Calories:
288 per portion

YOU WILL NEED:
500 g/1¼ lb smoked haddock
200 ml/7 fl oz skimmed milk
150 g/5 oz long-grain white rice
1 hard-boiled egg, chopped
100 g/4 oz peas, cooked
salt and pepper
parsley sprigs, to garnish

Poach the haddock in the milk for 10 minutes or until tender; drain, reserving the liquor. Flake the fish and remove any skin.

Cook the rice in plenty of boiling salted water for about 12 minutes, or until tender. Drain and rinse thoroughly, then return to the pan. Stir in the fish, eggs, peas and a little of the fish liquor. Season with salt and pepper to taste, then place over a low heat until heated through.

Transfer to a warmed serving dish and garnish with the parsley.

▨ COOK'S TIP

If you wish to use frozen cod-steaks, thaw them completely first. Pat them dry with absorbent kitchen paper before cooking.

▨ COOK'S TIP

This version of the traditional British breakfast dish is a good way to start the day for slimmers. You are much less likely to be tempted to nibble during the *morning! It is also a useful supper dish.*

57   STUFFED PEPPERS

Preparation time: 25 minutes	**YOU WILL NEED:** 500 g/1 ¼ lb cod fillets
	bouquet garni
Cooking time: 1¼ hours	½ onion
	salt and pepper
Oven temperature: 180°C, 350°F, gas 4	1 tablespoon sunflower oil
	1 onion, chopped
	2 celery sticks, chopped
Serves 4	100 g/4 oz brown rice
	1 x 225 g/8 oz can tomatoes
Calories: 303 per portion	1 bay leaf
	1 teaspoon chopped marjoram
	100 g/4 oz peeled cooked prawns
	4 tablespoons frozen sweetcorn
	4 green peppers (see Cook's Tip)
	whole cooked prawns

Put the fish in a pan with 300 ml/½ pint boiling water, bouquet garni, onion, and seasoning. Cover and simmer for 10-15 minutes. Remove with a slotted spoon, remove any skin and bones and flake into chunks.

Heat the oil in a frying pan, add the onion and celery and fry for 2 minutes. Add the rice and fry for 3 minutes. Stir in the tomatoes, their juice, bay leaf, marjoram, and seasoning to taste. Add 150 ml/¼ pint cold water, bring to the boil, cover and simmer for 40 minutes, until the rice is tender and the liquid absorbed. Remove from the heat. Stir in the fish, prawns and sweetcorn.

Divide the rice and fish mixture between the peppers. Arrange in an ovenproof dish and replace the reserved tops. Cook in the oven for 15 minutes. Garnish with the prawns.

■ COOK'S TIP

To prepare the peppers, remove the tops and reserve. Remove the cores and seeds. Blanch in boiling water 2 minutes, drain and plunge into cold water. Drain well.

58   TUNA-STUFFED GLOBE ARTICHOKES

Preparation time: 20 minutes, plus cooling	**YOU WILL NEED:** 4 globe artichokes
	salt
	100 g/4 oz long-grain rice
Cooking time: 25 minutes	1 x 350 g/12 oz can tuna fish in brine
	4 tablespoons tomato purée
Serves 4	2 teaspoons chopped fresh basil or 1 teaspoon dried basil
Calories: 212 per portion	2 teaspoons chopped fresh oregano or 1 teaspoon dried oregano
	salt and pepper

Cut off the artichoke stalks. Plunge the heads into boiling salted water. Simmer for about 20 minutes or until the bottom leaves pull away easily. Drain and leave until cold. Remove the hairy chokes from the centre of the artichokes.

Meanwhile, cook the rice in boiling salted water for about 12 minutes. Drain and leave for about 20 minutes, until cold.

Thoroughly drain the brine from the tuna fish and flake it using a fork. Add to the rice together with the tomato purée, herbs and salt and pepper to taste. Fill each globe artichoke with the tuna and rice mixture. Serve with a tomato salad.

■ COOK'S TIP

Avoid buying tuna fish canned in oil which will add unwanted calories. More rice could be cooked at the same time to be used in another dish the next day; *when cold, cover with cling film to prevent it hardening.*

59 FISH KEBABS

Preparation time:
15 minutes

Cooking time:
20 minutes

Serves 4

Calories:
114 per portion

YOU WILL NEED:
1 small green pepper, seeded and
   roughly chopped
450 g/1 lb cod, cut into small cubes
4 firm tomatoes, quartered
12 grapes, seeded
8 button mushrooms, trimmed
8 bay leaves
lemon juice
2 teaspoons chopped fresh tarragon or
   1 teaspoon dried

Put the chopped pepper in a saucepan and simmer in the minimum of water for 10 minutes. Drain.

Thread the fish cubes on to skewers with the tomato
quarters, grapes, mushrooms, pieces of pepper and bay
leaves. Sprinkle the kebabs with lemon juice and tarragon.
Place under a preheated moderate grill for about 10 minutes
until the fish is cooked, turning frequently and sprinkling with
more lemon juice if necessary.

60 COD SOFRITO

Preparation time:
15 minutes

Cooking time:
25-30 minutes

Serves 6

Calories:
217 per portion

YOU WILL NEED:
1 kg/2 ¼ lb cod fillet, skinned
4 tablespoons olive or corn oil
1 large onion, finely sliced
1 garlic clove, crushed
about 300 ml/½ pint fish stock
3 tablespoons lemon juice
½ teaspoon turmeric
1 x 5 cm/2 inch piece cinnamon stick
Maldon or sea salt
freshly ground white pepper
finely chopped parsley, to garnish

Rinse the cod fillet, then cut evenly into thin slices or cubes.

Heat the oil in a large pan, add the onion and cook gently
for 10 minutes until softened. Add the garlic and fry gently for
another 5 minutes. Add 150 ml/¼ pint of the fish stock, the
lemon juice and the turmeric. Bring just to the boil. Add the
fish, in one layer if possible, burying the cinnamon stick in the
middle. Sprinkle with salt and pepper, then simmer gently for
10-15 minutes, adding 2 tablespoons fish stock every 2-3
minutes and turning the fish once if it is in more than one
layer.

Pile on to a serving dish and sprinkle with plenty of
chopped parsley.

▇ COOK'S TIP

*These fish kebabs would be
good cooked over a
barbecue. Afterwards, rub
the grill with a cut lemon to
help get rid of any fishy
smell.*

▇ COOK'S TIP

*When the fish is just
cooked, taste the stock and
add an extra tablespoonful
of lemon juice if necessary.
Cod Sofrito is equally good
if left until cold, by which*

*time the liquid will have set
lightly to give a delicately
flavoured jelly.*

61 HERB KEDGEREE

Preparation time:
20 minutes

Cooking time:
1 hour 10 minutes

Serves 4

Calories:
340 per portion

YOU WILL NEED:
350 g/12 oz smoked haddock
25 g/1 oz soft margarine
1 onion, sliced
1 green pepper, seeded and sliced
175 g/6 oz brown long-grain rice,
  washed
grated rind and juice of 1 lemon
2 teaspoons dried mixed herbs
2 bay leaves
25 g/1 oz sultanas
100 g/4 oz peas, cooked
2 tablespoons chopped fresh herbs
salt and pepper
1 hard-boiled egg, sliced
lemon wedges
dill sprigs

Poach the smoked haddock in 450 ml/¾ pint water for 10 minutes, then remove fish and reserve stock. Remove the skin and any bones and flake the fish.

Melt the margarine in a large saucepan and sauté the onion and pepper for 2 minutes. Add the rice and cook for a further 2 minutes. Stir in the lemon rind, juice, herbs, bay leaves and reserved stock made up to 900 ml/1½ pints with water. Bring to the boil, cover and simmer for 40 minutes, or until most of the liquid is absorbed. Remove the bay leaves. Stir in the sultanas, peas and fish. Cook for a further 10 minutes, stirring occasionally. Add the fresh herbs and salt and pepper to taste. Transfer to a warmed serving dish. Garnish with the egg slices, lemon wedges and dill.

▉ COOK'S TIP

Some herbs are better suited to fish dishes than others. Try a mixture of lemon thyme, parsley, marjoram and chives in this kedgeree.

62 FISH CURRY

Preparation time:
15 minutes

Cooking time:
30-35 minutes

Serves 4

Calories:
216 per portion

YOU WILL NEED:
25 g/1 oz soft margarine
1 onion, chopped
½ green pepper, seeded and chopped
1 carrot, thinly sliced
2-3 teaspoons curry powder
1 tablespoon plain flour
300 ml/½ pint stock
1 teaspoon lemon juice
1 small apple, peeled, cored and
  chopped
1 tablespoon sultanas
500 g/1¼ lb haddock fillets, cut into
  cubes
salt and pepper
chopped parsley, to garnish

Melt the margarine in a pan and fry the onion, pepper, carrot and curry powder for 5 minutes. Stir in the flour and cook for 1 minute. Gradually blend in the stock and lemon juice. Heat, stirring until the sauce thickens. Add the apple, sultanas and haddock, then season to taste with salt and pepper. Cover and simmer for 20-25 minutes.

Transfer to a hot serving dish and garnish with the chopped parsley.

▉ COOK'S TIP

The amount of curry powder depends on your personal taste and on the type you are using. This curry should not be too fiery. Serve it with some *brown rice which has a nutty texture.*

63 HADDOCK AND CIDER CASSEROLE

Preparation time:
15 minutes

Cooking time:
40 minutes

Serves 4

Calories:
322 per portion

YOU WILL NEED:
1 large onion, sliced
2 celery sticks, thinly sliced
1 garlic clove, chopped
225 g/8 oz tomatoes, peeled and sliced
½ bunch watercress, chopped
3 medium potatoes, finely diced
300 ml/½ pint dry cider
2 tablespoons orange juice
strip of thinly pared orange rind
salt and pepper
750 g/1½ lb fresh haddock fillet,
    skinned and cut into 4-cm/
    1½-inch slices
watercress sprigs, to garnish
FOR THE TOPPING
5 tablespoons jumbo oats
40 g/1½ oz low-fat hard cheese, grated

Put the onion, celery, garlic and tomatoes into a flameproof casserole and cook over a low heat for 10 minutes. Add the watercress, potatoes, cider, orange juice and rind. Bring to the boil, cover and simmer for 10 minutes. Season, add the fish, cover and simmer for 10-12 minutes, or until it is just cooked. Discard the rind.

Mix together the oats and cheese and scatter over the dish. Cook under a preheated hot grill for 3 minutes, or until toasty-brown. Garnish with the watercress sprigs and serve hot with chilled low-fat yogurt.

▮ COOK'S TIP

Cider has fewer calories than wine and about the same as unsweetened apple juice. If you do not wish to use alcohol, replace the cider with apple juice.

64 BAKED MACKEREL IN CIDER

Preparation time:
15 minutes

Cooking time:
45 minutes

Oven temperature;
200°C, 400°F, gas
6; then 180°C,
350°F, gas 4

Serves 4

Calories:
460 per portion

YOU WILL NEED:
1 kg/2 lb cooking apples, peeled, cored
    and thinly sliced
5 tablespoons dry cider
150 g/5 oz natural low-fat yogurt
5 tablespoons Dijon mustard
salt and pepper
4 mackerel, filleted
FOR THE GARNISH
lemon slices
parsley sprigs

Spread the apples in a large lightly greased gratin dish.

Heat the cider gently and pour over the apples. Cover with foil and cook in a preheated moderately hot oven for 15 minutes. Lower the temperature to moderate.

Meanwhile, mix the yogurt with the mustard, and salt and pepper.

Arrange the mackerel in the dish and pour over the yogurt mixture. Return to the oven and cook for 30 minutes.

Garnish with lemon slices and parsley before serving.

▮ COOK'S TIP

The sharpness of the sauce makes a pleasant contrast to the slightly oily texture of the mackerel. Use one of the grainy Dijon mustards instead of a smooth variety.

65 SWEET AND SOUR MACKEREL

Preparation time:
20 minutes, plus marinating

Cooking time:
30 minutes

Oven temperature:
190°F, 375°F, gas 5

Serves 4

Calories:
400 per portion

YOU WILL NEED:
4 mackerel
FOR THE MARINADE
1 small onion, coarsely grated
1 carrot, coarsely grated
2 tablespoons white wine vinegar or lemon juice
1 tablespoon brown sugar
1 tablespoon soy sauce
salt and pepper
FOR THE GARNISH
25 g/1 oz blanched almonds, cut in shreds
lemon slices

Remove the heads and intestines from the mackerel and clean them well. Mix the vegetables with the other ingredients for the marinade and pour into a large dish. Place the mackerel in the mixture and leave for 1 hour, turning once or twice.

Lift the fish from the marinade; reserve this. Put the mackerel into an ovenproof dish and bake, uncovered, in the oven for 10 minutes. Pour the marinade over the fish, cover the dish and bake for a further 20 minutes. The vegetables should be slightly firm. Sprinkle the almonds over the fish just before serving. Garnish with lemon slices.

66 MUSHROOM-STUFFED PLAICE

Preparation time:
35 minutes

Cooking time:
35-40 minutes

Oven temperature:
200°C, 400°F, gas 6

Serves 4

Calories:
493 per portion

YOU WILL NEED:
4 whole plaice, cleaned
1 tablespoon oil
1 onion, finely chopped
1 garlic clove, crushed
75 g/3 oz fresh brown breadcrumbs
100 g/4 oz mushrooms, finely chopped
1 tomato, peeled and chopped
1 teaspoon chopped marjoram
2 teaspoons chopped parsley
dash of Worcestershire sauce
watercress sprigs, to garnish

Prepare the fish (see Cook's Tip). Heat the oil in a pan, add the onion, garlic and breadcrumbs and fry until the breadcrumbs are crisp. Stir in the remaining ingredients and sauté for 2 minutes. Divide the filling between the prepared pockets in the fish.

Place the fish in a buttered ovenproof dish and cover with foil. Cook in the oven for 20-30 minutes. Garnish with the watercress and serve immediately with grilled tomatoes and mushrooms.

■ COOK'S TIP

Budget-conscious cooks know that mackerel is both nutritious and much less expensive than some other fish. Ask your fishmonger to show you how to remove the intestines from the mackerel and clean them thoroughly.

■ COOK'S TIP

White side uppermost, make an incision down the backbone. On one half, cut two-thirds of the way around to form a pocket. Repeat on the other half.

67 MEDITERRANEAN FISH STEAKS

Preparation time:
15 minutes

Cooking time:
55 minutes

Oven temperature:
180°C, 350°F, gas 4

Serves 4

Calories:
251 per portion

YOU WILL NEED:
3 tablespoons olive oil
2 onions, thinly sliced
1 garlic clove, finely chopped
1 green pepper, seeded and sliced in rings
4 large tomatoes, peeled and sliced
2 teaspoons dried basil
salt and pepper
4 white fish steaks, about 175 g/ 6 oz each
2 teaspoons lemon juice
4 tablespoons dry white wine
2 tablespoons water

Heat the oil in a frying pan and fry the onions and garlic until softened. Add the green pepper rings and continue frying for 3 minutes. Remove from the heat and place half the mixture, discarding any oil, in a casserole.

Arrange half the tomato slices on top and sprinkle with half the basil and salt and pepper to taste. Place the fish steaks on top and sprinkle with the lemon juice. Add the remaining tomato slices, basil and onion mixture. Pour in the wine and water. Cover and cook in the oven for about 45 minutes, or until the fish is tender.

68 PIQUANT PLAICE

Preparation time:
20 minutes

Cooking time:
13 minutes

Serves 4

Calories:
247 per portion

YOU WILL NEED:
8 small plaice fillets, skinned, about 65 g/2 ½ oz each
salt and pepper
¼ teaspoon ground ginger
1 small onion, finely chopped
150 ml/¼ pint white wine
150 ml/¼ pint chicken stock
2 green leeks, cleaned and cut into matchstick strips
4 tablespoons low-calorie mayonnaise
4 tablespoons natural low-fat yogurt
1 thin slice fresh root ginger
½ teaspoon mild curry powder
small croûtons, to garnish (see Cook's Tip)

Lay the plaice fillets down, skinned sides uppermost, and sprinkle with salt, pepper and ginger. Roll up and secure with wooden cocktail sticks. Scatter the onion in a large frying pan; lay the plaice on top and add the white wine and stock. Cover the pan and simmer gently for about 10 minutes. Meanwhile simmer the strips of leek in boiling water for 3 minutes.

Remove the plaice paupiettes and keep warm. Place the drained strips of leek around the fish.

Mix the mayonnaise with the yogurt. Squeeze the root ginger in a garlic press to extract the juice and add to the mixture with the curry powder and seasonings. Arrange two paupiettes on each plate and garnish with the strips of leek and croûtons. Serve the sauce separately.

■ COOK'S TIP

Any firm, white fish steaks are suitable for this appetizing dish. Ask your fishmonger's advice about the best buy at any particular time of the year and freeze the fish to use later.

■ COOK'S TIP

The croûtons for this dish are made by stamping out crescents from thinly sliced bread and toasting them slowly until crisp.

69 MACKEREL PARCELS

Preparation time:
20 minutes

Cooking time:
35-45 minutes

Oven temperature:
180°C, 350°F, gas 4

Serves 6

Calories:
455 per portion

YOU WILL NEED:

6 small mackerel, about 275 g/
   10 oz each, cleaned but heads
   and tails left on
Maldon or sea salt
freshly ground white pepper
275 g/10 oz gooseberries, topped and
   tailed
½ teaspoon sugar (optional)
1 teaspoon lemon juice
40 g/1½ oz hazelnuts, finely chopped
¼ teaspoon green peppercorns,
   drained if in brine, lightly crushed
6 tablespoons dry cider
coriander sprigs, to garnish

Rinse the mackerel, rubbing any traces of blood with a little salt. Rub salt and pepper over the fish; set aside.

To make the stuffing, put the gooseberries into a small pan and add just enough cold water to cover. Bring to the boil, then simmer gently for 10-20 minutes until soft and pulpy and most of the liquid has been absorbed. Taste and add sugar if necessary. Stir in the lemon juice, nuts and peppercorns.

Cut out six pieces of foil, each large enough to enclose the fish with a good edge left to seal the parcels. Stuff each fish, pushing the mixture through the belly cavity. Put each fish on a piece of foil. Sprinkle a tablespoon of cider over each, grind over some white pepper, then seal the parcels tightly. Cook in the oven for 20-25 minutes. Open the parcels and garnish.

70 CHINESE STEAMED TROUT

Preparation time:
15 minutes

Cooking time:
15 minutes

Serves 4

Calories:
440 per portion

YOU WILL NEED:

1 teaspoon sesame oil
1 tablespoon light soy sauce
1 tablespoon dry sherry
2 rainbow trout, about 1 kg/2¼ lb
   total weight, cleaned
4 garlic cloves, thinly sliced
6 spring onions, shredded
2 × 2.5 cm/1 inch pieces root ginger,
   shredded
2 tablespoons dry white vermouth
2 tablespoons oil

Mix together the sesame oil, soy sauce and sherry and use to brush the inside and the skin of each fish.

Mix together the garlic, spring onions and ginger and place a quarter of the mixture inside each fish. Put the fish on a heatproof plate, scatter over the remaining garlic mixture and pour over the vermouth and oil. Put the plate in a wok and steam vigorously for 15 minutes, or until the fish is tender.

Arrange the fish on a warmed serving plate, spoon over the juices and serve immediately.

■ COOK'S TIP

The fish may be prepared, and the stuffing cooked, up to 3 hours in advance, if covered with cling film and kept cool until you are ready to cook it. On a very *hot day, chill the fish and bring to room temperature before stuffing.*

■ COOK'S TIP

If you do not have a wok, put the plate on a grill rack in a roasting tin half-filled with water and cover with foil, to make a tent over the fish.

71 RED MULLET WITH CORIANDER SEEDS

Preparation time:
10 minutes, plus standing

Cooking time:
10-12 minutes

Serves 6

Calories:
240 per portion

YOU WILL NEED:
6 *small red mullet, cleaned, livers not removed*
3 *tablespoons olive oil*
2 *tablespoons coriander seeds, lightly crushed*
3-4 *garlic cloves, finely chopped*
Maldon or sea salt
freshly ground white pepper
FOR THE GARNISH
lemon slices
bay leaves

Rinse the mullet quickly and pat dry with absorbent kitchen paper. Brush with 1 tablespoon of the oil and leave for 5 minutes.

Heat the remaining oil in a frying pan, add the coriander seeds and garlic and fry for 2 minutes. Brush the fish with some of this mixture, sprinkle with salt and pepper, and cook under a hot grill for 4-5 minutes. Turn and brush with the remaining oil, then grill for 4-5 minutes until crisp. Garnish and serve immediately.

72 PLAICE WITH COURGETTE AND LEMON SAUCE

Preparation time:
25 minutes

Cooking time:
15 minutes

Serves 4

Calories:
169 per portion

YOU WILL NEED:
8 *small plaice fillets, about 65 g/2 ½ oz each, skinned*
salt and pepper
finely grated rind of ½ lemon
1 *tablespoon finely chopped parsley*
300 *ml/½ pint skimmed milk*
FOR THE SAUCE
350 *g/12 oz courgettes*
300 *ml/½ pint chicken stock*
grated rind of ½ lemon
1 *garlic clove, chopped*
dill sprigs, to garnish

Spread out the plaice fillets, skinned sides uppermost. Sprinkle with salt and pepper to taste, lemon rind and parsley, and roll each one up, securing with a wooden cocktail stick.

For the sauce, chop the courgettes and cook with the stock, lemon rind and garlic until just tender. Blend the cooked courgettes and their liquid until smooth.

Put the rolled plaice fillets into a shallow pan; add the milk and salt and pepper to taste. Poach the fish gently until it is just tender, about 8-10 minutes, then drain, reserving the liquid. Put on a warmed serving dish.

Heat the courgette purée in a pan with sufficient of the fish cooking liquid to make a fairly thin sauce. Spoon the sauce around the rolled fish fillets and garnish with dill.

■ COOK'S TIP

Ideally crush the coriander seeds in a pestle and mortar. Otherwise, try covering the seeds with a piece of greaseproof paper and pressing them with a heavy *rolling pin to release their fragrance.*

■ COOK'S TIP

Thinly sliced courgettes are an ideal vegetable to serve with plaice. Poach them gently in chicken stock until they are just tender while the fish is cooking.

73 RED MULLET WITH CHICORY

Preparation time:
20 minutes

Cooking time:
35 minutes

Oven temperature:
180°C, 350°F, gas 4

Serves 4

Calories:
247 per portion

YOU WILL NEED:
350 g/12 oz chicory
salt and pepper
25 g/1 oz unsalted butter
1 small onion, sliced
1 shallot, finely sliced
2 teaspoons lemon juice
salt and pepper
4 small red mullet, cleaned and scaled
FOR THE GARNISH
dill sprigs
lemon wedges

Blanch the chicory in boiling salted water for 5 minutes. Drain, then break off and slice the leaves.

Melt the butter in a pan, stir in the onion, shallot, chicory, lemon juice, and salt and pepper to taste. Cover and cook for 5 minutes.

Spoon into an ovenproof dish. Place the red mullet on top and sprinkle with salt and pepper. Cover with foil and cook in the oven for 20 minutes, or until cooked. Garnish with dill and lemon to serve.

74 FISH PLAKI

Preparation time:
15 minutes, plus cooling

Cooking time:
40-45 minutes

Oven temperature:
180°C, 350°F, gas 4

Serves 4

Calories:
313 per portion

YOU WILL NEED:
1 kg/2¼ lb fish fillets, cut into fairly thick slices
1 large lemon
3 large onions, thinly sliced
2-3 garlic cloves, finely chopped
¾ teaspoon fresh oregano
3 beefsteak tomatoes, peeled and thinly sliced
4 tablespoons finely chopped parsley
Maldon or sea salt
freshly ground black pepper
2 tablespoons olive oil
about 300 ml/½ pint water

Arrange the fish in an ovenproof dish. Grate the lemon rind evenly over the fish, then peel off all the pith and cut the flesh into slices. Lay on top of the fish. Add the onion slices, garlic and oregano. Top with the tomatoes and sprinkle over the parsley, salt and plenty of pepper. Mix the oil with the water and pour over the fish. The liquid should just cover all the ingredients, so add a little more water if necessary.

Bake in the oven for 40-45 minutes, or until a fork penetrates the fish very easily. Cool to room temperature (about 25 minutes).

■ COOK'S TIP

Buy the chicory on the same day as you are making the dish if possible. The outer leaves tend to discolour soon and lose their crispness.

■ COOK'S TIP

John Dory is a delicious fish to choose for this Greek dish. Oregano is the best substitute for the rigani used in Greece. This mixture of dried flowers and leaves of marjoram is not obtainable elsewhere.

75 STEAMED TROUT WITH YOGURT

Preparation time:
20 minutes

Cooking time:
10-15 minutes

Serves 4

Calories:
275 per portion

YOU WILL NEED:
4 trout, gutted and cleaned
4 tablespoons lemon juice
1 tablespoon chopped parsley
1 teaspoon dried thyme
freshly ground black pepper
FOR THE SAUCE
150 ml/¼ pint natural low-fat yogurt
2 tablespoons grated horseradish or
    horseradish sauce
2 tablespoons lemon juice
1 teaspoon white wine vinegar
½ teaspoon dried tarragon
1 teaspoon chopped chives
pinch of cayenne
FOR THE GARNISH
flat leaf parsley
chives

Put the trout on a large sheet of foil and sprinkle with lemon juice, parsley, thyme and black pepper. Fold into a parcel and place between two large plates. Put these over a pan of boiling water and allow to steam for 10-15 minutes, or until tender. Transfer to a warmed dish.

To make the sauce, put the yogurt, horseradish, lemon juice, vinegar, tarragon, chives and cayenne in a heatproof bowl. Put over a pan of simmering water and stir until hot and creamy. Pour over the trout and serve immediately, garnished with the parsley and chives.

■ COOK'S TIP

*Serve boiled new potatoes
with the trout. With the
creamy yogurt sauce, you
will not be tempted to put
any butter on the potatoes!*

76 SOLE VERONICA

Preparation time:
15 minutes

Cooking time:
20 minutes

Serves 4

Calories:
141 per portion

YOU WILL NEED:
4 sole fillets, about 100 g/4 oz each
250 ml/8 fl oz grape juice
salt and pepper
40 grapes, seeded

Put the sole fillets in a wide shallow pan and pour over the grape juice. Season with salt and pepper. Simmer gently for about 15 minutes until the fish is tender. Add the grapes and cook for a further 5 minutes. Transfer the fish to a warmed serving dish and pour the sauce and grapes over.

■ COOK'S TIP

*Both red and white grape
juice are available in large
supermarkets and health
food shops. It is important
to read the label carefully to
make sure it does not* *contain any form of
sweetening.*

77 SEABASS BAKED WITH MANGETOUT

Preparation time:	**YOU WILL NEED:**
5 minutes	75 g/3 oz unsalted butter
	1.5 kg/3 lb seabass, cleaned, head and
Cooking time:	tail cut off, fish boned
45 minutes	300 ml/½ pint dry white wine
Oven temperature:	3-4 garlic cloves, finely chopped
190°C, 375°F, gas 5	½ teaspoon ground cinnamon
	Maldon or sea salt
Serves 6	freshly ground black pepper
Calories:	6 tablespoons finely chopped parsley
338 per portion	350 g/12 oz mangetout
	3-4 tablespoons lemon juice
	lemon twists, to garnish

Rub a large ovenproof serving dish with a little of the butter, then place the seabass in it, leaving room on either side to add the mangetout. Cut the remaining butter into small pieces and dot all over the fish, then pour over the wine and sprinkle with the garlic, cinnamon, salt and plenty of pepper, finally covering with the parsley. Lay on a butter paper and cook in the oven for 40 minutes.

Meanwhile blanch the mangetout for 30 seconds in boiling water. Remove the butter paper, put the mangetout around the seabass, spooning a little of the melted butter over them. Sprinkle both the fish and the mangetout with lemon juice and bake for another 5-6 minutes until the mangetout are just cooked but still crunchy and the fish flakes easily when tested with a fork. Garnish and serve immediately.

■ COOK'S TIP

Bream or grey mullet can also be cooked in this way. Although mangetout are available all the year round, they are best value in summer.

78 PIKE WITH BEETROOT SAUCE

Preparation time:	**YOU WILL NEED:**
15 minutes, plus	1 pike, weighing about 2 kg/4½ lb,
marinating	gutted, scaled and cleaned
	juice of 1 lemon
Cooking time:	salt and pepper
45-50 minutes	50 g/2 oz rindless back bacon
Oven temperature:	1 bunch mixed fresh herbs
190°C, 375°F, gas 5	40 g/1½ oz margarine
	250 g/9 oz cooked beetroot
Serves 6	4 tablespoons dry red wine
Calories:	1 teaspoon sugar
400 per portion	herbs, to garnish

Wash the pike, wipe dry with absorbent kitchen paper and sprinkle inside and out with lemon juice. Leave the fish to marinate for about 10 minutes, then season with salt and pepper to taste.

Make deep cuts on each side of the fish with a sharp knife and fill each cut with a slice of bacon. Stuff the fish with the herbs. Place the fish in a large roasting tin and dot with 25 g/ 1 oz of the margarine. Cook in the oven for 45-50 minutes.

Meanwhile, to make the sauce, purée the beetroot in a liquidizer with the red wine. Transfer to a small pan and heat gently. Stir in the remaining margarine, sugar, and salt and pepper to taste. Arrange the fish on a warmed platter, garnish with herbs and serve with the sauce.

■ COOK'S TIP

Pike is often caught by anglers, but it may be difficult to find in a fishmonger. Another oily fish, such as salmon trout, could be used instead.

79 SWORDFISH PROVENCAL

Preparation time:
20 minutes, plus
marinating

Cooking time:
45-50 minutes

Oven temperature:
180°C, 350°F, gas 4

Serves 4

Calories:
191 per portion

YOU WILL NEED:
2 swordfish steaks
1 tablespoon sunflower oil
1 onion, sliced
750 g/1½ lb tomatoes, thickly sliced
250 g/9 oz green beans, cut in half
100 g/4 oz green olives, stoned
2 tablespoons capers
2 teaspoons chopped fresh oregano
FOR THE MARINADE
150 ml/¼ pint dry white wine
4 tablespoons lemon juice
1 small onion, sliced
1 bay leaf
2 thyme sprigs
2 parsley sprigs
2 rosemary sprigs
2 garlic cloves, crushed
salt and pepper

Cut the swordfish steaks in half, place in a shallow dish and add the marinade ingredients. Chill for 5 hours.

Remove the fish with a slotted spoon; reserve the marinade. Heat the oil in a large pan, add the fish and fry for 5 minutes. Transfer to a casserole. Add the onion, tomatoes, beans, olives, capers, oregano and reserved marinade to the pan and cook, stirring for 5 minutes. Transfer to the casserole and season. Cook in the oven for 35-40 minutes. Discard the bay leaf.

80 HALIBUT WITH TARRAGON

Preparation time:
10 minutes, plus
marinating

Cooking time:
15-20 minutes

Oven temperature:
200°C, 400°F, gas 6

Serves 4

Calories:
180 per portion

YOU WILL NEED:
4 halibut steaks, about 175 g/6 oz
    each
grated rind and juice of 2-3 lemons
few tarragon sprigs
salt and pepper

Place the halibut in a large shallow dish. Sprinkle over the lemon rind and juice, tarragon, salt and pepper. Turn the fish to coat with the mixture. Cover and leave to marinate for about 3 hours.

Place each piece of fish on a sheet of foil large enough to enclose it. Spoon over a little of the marinade and wrap up the fish. Cook in the oven for about 15-20 minutes, depending on the thickness of the halibut. Unwrap and serve on a warmed dish.

▉ COOK'S TIP

*So called because of its long
sword-like beak, swordfish
is delicious but is inclined to
be dry, so marinating it
before cooking is a good
way to use it.*

▉ COOK'S TIP

*Rinse the halibut steaks in
cold water to remove any
blood, rubbing with a little
salt if necessary. Cod steaks
can also be cooked in the
same way.*

81 BAKED HALIBUT WITH FENNEL

Preparation time:
10 minutes

Cooking time:
30-35 minutes

Oven temperature:
180°C, 350°F, gas 4

Serves 4

Calories:
454 per portion

YOU WILL NEED:
6 halibut steaks, about 175 g/6 oz
   each, rinsed
2 large fennel bulbs, finely sliced,
   leaves chopped
40 g/1½ oz butter
2-3 garlic cloves, crushed
100 ml/3½ fl oz dry vermouth
Maldon or sea salt
freshly ground black pepper

Blanch the fennel bulbs in a large pan of boiling water for 2 minutes, then drain thoroughly. Melt the butter, add the fennel bulbs and garlic and cook gently for 10 minutes, or until softened. Spread the fennel, with its butter, over the base of an ovenproof casserole, then add the fish. Pour the vermouth, with a little salt and plenty of pepper, over the fish.

Cook in the oven for 18-25 minutes, until the fish just flakes easily. Serve at once, sprinkled with chopped fennel leaves.

82 CITRUS HALIBUT STEAK

Preparation time:
10 minutes, plus
marinating

Cooking time:
20 minutes

Oven temperature:
180°C, 350°F, gas 4

Serves 2

Calories:
215 per portion

YOU WILL NEED:
grated rind and juice of 1 orange
grated rind and juice of 1 lemon
grated rind and juice of 1 lime
1 halibut steak, cut in half
FOR THE GARNISH
2 orange slices
2 lemon slices
2 lime slices

Place 1 tablespoon of each grated rind and all the fruit juices in an ovenproof dish. Add the fish and baste well. Cover and chill for 12 hours, turning the steaks over after 6 hours.

Cover the dish with foil and cook in the oven for 20 minutes. Garnish each portion with an orange, lemon and lime slice.

COOK'S TIP

*The cooking time varies
depending on the thickness
of the halibut steaks. Fish
should never be overcooked
so check if the halibut is
ready after 18 minutes.*

COOK'S TIP

*Prepare this dish sufficiently
early in the day to allow
time for it to marinate. As
the steaks are turned after 6
hours, it is not practical to
marinate them overnight!*

83 TANDOORI SOLE

Preparation time:
10 minutes, plus
marinating

Cooking time:
15 minutes

Oven temperature:
180°C, 350°F, gas 4

Serves 4

Calories:
184 per portion

YOU WILL NEED:
½ teaspoon chilli powder
½ teaspoon turmeric
½ teaspoon ground coriander
½ teaspoon ground cumin
1 teaspoon ground ginger
½ teaspoon garam masala
¼ teaspoon salt
300 ml/½ pint natural low-fat yogurt
2 garlic cloves, crushed
4 lemon sole, skinned and filleted
FOR THE GARNISH
coriander leaves
lime wedges

Mix all the spices together. Add to the yogurt with the garlic and stir until well mixed. Pour into a large bowl, add the fish, turn to coat thoroughly and leave to marinate for 1 hour.

Pour boiling water into a roasting pan to come halfway up the sides. Put a grill rack in the pan and place the marinated fish on the rack. Pour any remaining marinade over the fish. Cook in the oven for 15 minutes. Garnish with coriander and lime wedges and serve immediately.

84 SEABASS BAKED IN SPINACH

Preparation time:
30 minutes

Cooking time:
30 minutes

Oven temperature:
200°C, 400°F, gas 6

Serves 4

Calories:
400 per portion

YOU WILL NEED:
1 seabass, weighing about 750 g/
1½ lb, cleaned and gutted
250 g/9 oz spinach
2 shallots, chopped
150 ml/¼ pint dry white wine
3 orange slices, quartered, to garnish
FOR THE STUFFING
50 g/2 oz fresh breadcrumbs
15 g/½ oz butter, melted
2 tablespoons chopped chervil
1 tablespoon chopped tarragon
1 tablespoon chopped basil
1 tablespoon lemon juice
salt and pepper

Mix the stuffing ingredients together, seasoning with salt and pepper to taste, and use to stuff the fish cavity.

Put the spinach in a colander in a bowl and pour over boiling water. Drain thoroughly. Wrap the stuffed seabass in the blanched spinach, leaving the head and tail exposed. Sprinkle the shallots over the base of a gratin dish and place the fish on top. Pour over the wine. Cover with foil and cook in the oven for 30 minutes.

Transfer to a warmed serving dish and garnish with quartered orange slices.

■ COOK'S TIP

Garam masala is an aromatic mixture of Oriental spices. It is best to buy it in a shop with a brisk turnover of seasonings used in ethnic cooking.

■ COOK'S TIP

The seabass should be really fresh. In choosing it you should look for firmness of flesh, brightness of eye and gleaming skin with its beautiful markings.

85 SOLE FILLETS WITH SOY AND GINGER

Preparation time:
15 minutes, plus
chilling

Cooking time:
10 minutes

Serves 6

Calories:
171 per portion

YOU WILL NEED:
750 g/1½ sole fillets, skinned
2 egg whites
1 teaspoon cornflour
½ teaspoon Maldon or sea salt
3 tablespoons peanut or grapeseed oil
1 x 5 cm/2 inch piece fresh root
    ginger, peeled and grated
1 large garlic clove, very finely
    chopped
3 tablespoons soy sauce
1 tablespoon dry sherry
3 tablespoons fish stock
3 spring onions, cut into matchstick
    strips

Cut the sole into long thin strips. Beat the egg whites, corn-flour and salt until frothy, then pour over the fish, mixing well. Chill for 20 minutes.

Heat the oil in a wok or large frying pan. When nearly smoking, add the fish and stir-fry over a fairly high heat for 2 minutes. Remove from the pan with a slotted spoon, then discard all but 1 tablespoon of the oil. Add the ginger and garlic and stir-fry for 1 minute, then pour in the soy sauce, sherry and fish stock. Bring to the boil quickly, then bubble for 2 minutes. Return the fish to the pan and heat through for 1 minute, stirring constantly. Pile on to a warmed serving dish, sprinkling with the spring onion strips and serve at once.

■ COOK'S TIP

Dip your fingers in cold water and then in salt before you start to skin the sole fillets. Serve the fillets with lightly cooked baby corn-cobs.

86 POACHED SALMON TROUT

Preparation time:
35-40 minutes, plus
chilling

Cooking time:
30 minutes

Oven temperature:
150°C, 300°F, gas 2

Serves 6

Calories:
341 per portion

YOU WILL NEED:
1 salmon trout, weighing about
    1 kg/2¼ lb, cleaned and gutted
1 bay leaf
1 lemon, sliced
1 teaspoon salt
12 black peppercorns
300 ml/½ pint dry white wine
FOR THE GARNISH
½ x 25 g/1 oz packet aspic powder
2 lemons, sliced
2 limes, sliced
small bunch of dill
½ packet of watercress

Line a large roasting pan with foil and brush lightly with the oil. Place the salmon trout on the foil, curving the fish slightly. Place the bay leaf and lemon slices on the fish, then sprinkle with the salt and peppercorns. Pour over the wine. Bring the edges of foil together and seal.

Cook in the oven for 30 minutes. Leave to cool in the pan. Unwrap the fish, remove the skin, leaving some around the head and tail, and place on a serving dish.

Make up the aspic to 300 ml/½ pint according to packet directions. Coat the fish with a thin layer of aspic jelly. Cut most of the lemon and lime slices into quarters and arrange down the centre of the fish with the dill. Brush the lemon and lime slices with a little aspic jelly. Chill in the refrigerator until set (about 2½ hours). Garnish with any remaining lemon and lime slices and watercress.

■ COOK'S TIP

If you do not have a fish kettle, this is the best way of poaching a salmon trout. Allow the coating of aspic jelly to set slightly before adding the citrus slices.

87 POACHED SALMON STEAKS WITH HOT BASIL SAUCE

Preparation time:
15 minutes

Cooking time:
25 minutes

Serves 6

Calories:
241 per portion

YOU WILL NEED:
1 large bunch fresh basil
4 celery sticks, chopped
1 carrot, chopped
1 small courgette, chopped
1 small onion, chopped
6 salmon steaks, about 100 g/4 oz
each and 2.5 cm/1 inch thick
85 ml/3 fl oz dry white wine
120 ml/4 fl oz water
salt and pepper
1 teaspoon lemon juice
15 g/½ oz unsalted butter

Strip the leaves off half the basil and set aside. Spread all the chopped vegetables over the bottom of a large flameproof dish with a lid, press the salmon steaks into the vegetables and cover them with the remaining basil. Pour over the wine and water and add salt and pepper to taste. Bring to the boil, cover and simmer for about 10 minutes. Transfer the salmon to a warmed serving dish.

Bring the poaching liquid and vegetables back to the boil and simmer for 5 minutes. Strain into a liquidizer and add the cooked and uncooked basil. Blend to a purée and return to a saucepan. Bring the purée to the boil and reduce by half, until thickened. Remove the pan from the heat, add the lemon juice and stir in the butter. Pour the sauce over the salmon steaks and serve.

■ COOK'S TIP

Make sure that you do not overcook the salmon. It should be opaque and firm when tested with the point of a sharp knife.

88 CREAMED COCONUT MONKFISH

Preparation time:
20 minutes, plus
infusing

Cooking time:
10-15 minutes

Serves 4

Calories:
360 per portion

YOU WILL NEED:
100 g/4 oz desiccated coconut
300 ml/½ pint boiling water
750 g/1½ lb monkfish
1 tablespoon oil
6 spring onions, chopped
3 green chillies, seeded and chopped
1 red pepper, seeded and chopped
1 garlic clove, crushed
1 x 5 cm/2 inch piece fresh root
ginger, chopped
½ teaspoon ground cumin
½ teaspoon ground coriander
1 teaspoon grated lemon rind
1 tablespoon lime juice
1 tablespoon dry sherry
salt and pepper
FOR THE GARNISH
lime wedges
coriander leaves

Put the coconut in a bowl, pour over the boiling water and leave to infuse for 30 minutes. Strain and reserve the liquid, discarding the coconut.

Meanwhile, cut the fish into 5 cm/2 inch cubes. Heat the oil in a large pan and stir in the remaining ingredients. Add the fish, pour on the coconut milk and bring to the boil, then simmer for 5 minutes. Transfer to a warmed serving dish and garnish with lime and coriander.

■ COOK'S TIP

Monkfish is also known as angler fish. Unfortunately it tends to be rather expensive. It is also delicious when grilled and served cold with an avocado salad.

89 FISH CASSEROLE

Preparation time:
45 minutes

Cooking time:
30-35 minutes

Serves 6

Calories:
278 per portion

YOU WILL NEED:

12 mussels, cleaned

salt and pepper

1 monkfish, cleaned and filleted

2 squid, cleaned

2 onions, chopped

2 carrots, thinly sliced

6 celery sticks, sliced

2 garlic cloves, crushed

1 x 400 g/14 oz can tomatoes

2 teaspoons sugar

2 tablespoons lemon juice

2 tablespoons lime juice

2 tablespoons chopped coriander

bouquet garni

150 ml/¼ pint dry cider

few drops Tabasco

4 scallops, cleaned and cut in half
    horizontally

3 small red mullet, cleaned

Cook the mussels in boiling salted water about 7 minutes; discard any that do not open. Cut the monkfish into chunks. Cut the squid into slices; leave the tentacles in small pieces.

Heat 2 tablespoons oil in a large saucepan, add the onions, carrots, celery and garlic and sauté for 4 minutes. Add the remaining ingredients, except the fish, with salt and pepper to taste, and bring to the boil. Add all the fish except the mussels, cover and simmer for 15-20 minutes, until the fish is cooked. Discard the bouquet garni. Stir in the mussels and transfer to a warmed serving dish.

▌COOK'S TIP

A wonderful casserole to make if you are lucky enough to have an enterprising fishmonger who can supply all the different types of fish and shellfish.

You may have to order the squid in advance.

90 SCALLOPS PROVENCAL

Preparation time:
15-20 minutes

Cooking time:
5 minutes

Serves 4

Calories:
297 per portion

YOU WILL NEED:

8 large scallops

Maldon or sea salt

freshly ground black pepper

3 tablespoons lemon juice

65 g/2 ½ oz unsalted butter

1 tablespoon olive oil

4 tablespoons home-made dried
    breadcrumbs

2 garlic cloves, finely chopped

3 tablespoons finely chopped parsley

Prepare the scallops (see Cook's Tip), cut each one in half horizontally and put the discs into a shallow bowl, sprinkle them lightly with salt and black pepper, then pour over the lemon juice.

Melt 25 g/1 oz of the butter in a large frying pan, add the oil, then the breadcrumbs and fry gently for 2-3 minutes until lightly crisp and golden. Tip the breadcrumbs into a bowl and reserve. Wipe the pan clean with absorbent kitchen paper and return to the heat. Melt the remaining butter and when just starting to bubble, add the scallop discs and fry for 1-2 minutes. Stir in the finely chopped garlic and parsley, then add the corals and continue cooking for another minute. Mix in the breadcrumbs, then quickly divide between the shells or small serving dishes and serve immediately.

▌COOK'S TIP

To prepare the scallops, detach from the shells, separating the coral from the white flesh. Cut off and discard any black pieces and the greyish gristle.

91 TURBOT AND PRAWN CREOLE

Preparation time:
15 minutes

Cooking time:
35-40 minutes

Serves 4

Calories:
160 per portion

YOU WILL NEED:
1 onion, chopped
1 green pepper, seeded and chopped
1 x 400 g/14 oz can tomatoes
½ teaspoon basil
½ teaspoon oregano
pinch of sugar
salt and pepper
250 g/9 oz turbot, cut into cubes
250 g/9 oz peeled, cooked prawns
2 teaspoons cornflour
2 tablespoons dry white wine
FOR THE GARNISH
whole cooked prawns
chopped parsley

Put the onion, green pepper, tomatoes and their juice, basil, oregano and sugar in a saucepan. Add salt and pepper to taste. Bring to the boil, cover and simmer for 15 minutes.

Add the turbot and prawns and simmer for a further 10-15 minutes. Blend the cornflour and wine until smooth, then stir into the sauce. Heat until the sauce thickens and continue cooking for 2 minutes.

Transfer to a hot serving dish and garnish with whole prawns and chopped parsley.

92 STIR-FRIED CRAB AND SOLE

Preparation time:
25 minutes

Cooking time:
7-10 minutes

Serves 4

Calories:
388 per portion

YOU WILL NEED:
25 g/1 oz butter
2 tablespoons olive oil
1 small onion, finely chopped
1 garlic clove, crushed
2 leeks, cleaned and cut into julienne
    strips (see Cook's Tip)
350 g/12 oz sole fillets, skinned and
    cut into thin strips
225 g/8 oz white crabmeat, flaked
4 tablespoons chicken stock
1 small avocado, peeled, halved,
    stoned and sliced
1 teaspoon grated lemon rind
salt
1 teaspoon green peppercorns in brine,
    drained
2 tablespoons finely chopped fresh
    parsley or dill, to garnish

Heat the butter and oil in a wok or large frying pan and gently fry the onion and garlic for 3 minutes. Add the julienne strips of leek and the strips of sole, and stir-fry gently until the fish is opaque.

Add the crabmeat, stock, avocado slices, lemon rind, salt and peppercorns; stir-fry for 2-3 minutes. Serve immediately, sprinkled with parsley or dill.

▌ COOK'S TIP

A less expensive white fish than turbot can be substituted. Supermarkets often reduce the price of peeled, cooked prawns on a Saturday afternoon as they would no longer be fresh on Monday.

▌ COOK'S TIP

Wash and dry the leeks thoroughly before cutting them into julienne strips. Use a sharp knife to cut even strips about 5 cm/2 inches long.

93 PRAWN AND SPINACH PILAU

Preparation time:
15 minutes

Cooking time:
50-55 minutes

Serves 6

Calories:
320 per portion

YOU WILL NEED:
750 g/1 lb cooked prawns in their
  shells
2 x 5 cm/2 inch pieces lemon peel
3 parsley sprigs
1 thyme sprig
6 white peppercorns, crushed
1.2 litres/2 pints water
750 g/1½ lb spinach, washed
350 g/12 oz long-grain rice
3 tablespoons olive oil
2 large onions, finely chopped
1 garlic clove, crushed
freshly grated nutmeg
Maldon or sea salt

Make the prawn stock (see Cook's Tip). Shred the spinach finely. Measure and note the volume of rice, rinse in boiling water and soak in fresh boiled water for 5 minutes.

Heat the oil in a large saucepan, add the onion and cook gently for about 5 minutes, until starting to soften. Add the garlic and spinach, and stir-fry for 2-3 minutes. Drain the rice and add to the pan, stirring until it gleams with a light coating of oil, then grate over a generous amount of nutmeg. Measure out the same volume of prawn stock as the rice and pour over the rice. Season well, bring quickly to the boil, bubble for 10 seconds, then reduce the heat, add the prawns, cover and cook for 15-20 minutes until the liquid is absorbed. Turn off the heat, stir, then cover the pan and leave for 5 minutes.

▥ COOK'S TIP

To make the prawn stock, shell the prawns and put their heads and shells into a large pan with the lemon peel, herbs and peppercorns. Add the cold water and bring to the boil, then simmer for 20 minutes. Strain.

94 PRAWNS IN GINGER SAUCE

Preparation time:
10 minutes

Cooking time:
6-7 minutes

Serves 4

Calories:
85 per portion

YOU WILL NEED:
8 spring onions, chopped
1 x 5 cm/2 inch piece fresh root
  ginger, chopped
2 tablespoons dry sherry
2 tablespoons soy sauce
150 ml/¼ pint chicken stock
salt and pepper
12 peeled, cooked Mediterranean
  prawns

Put all the ingredients, except the prawns, in a saucepan, seasoning with salt and pepper to taste. Bring to the boil, then simmer for 2 minutes.

Stir in the prawns, cover and cook for 3 minutes. Serve immediately.

▥ COOK'S TIP

Noodles are the traditional accompaniment to this dish. Cook some fresh egg noodles for 1 minute in boiling salted water.

95 PRAWNS WITH ALMONDS

Preparation time:
25 minutes

Cooking time:
4-6 minutes

Serves 4

Calories:
232 per portion

YOU WILL NEED:
75 g/3 oz blanched almonds
350 g/12 oz peeled, cooked prawns
2 teaspoons cornflour
1 teaspoon finely chopped fresh root
  ginger
1 small garlic clove, crushed
2 tablespoons oil
1 celery stick, finely chopped
2 teaspoons soy sauce
2 teaspoons dry sherry
2 tablespoons water
pepper
spring onion flowers, to garnish

Brush a frying pan lightly with oil, add the almonds, then heat and toss until golden; be careful not to let them burn. Drain on absorbent kitchen paper.

Put the prawns in a basin with the cornflour, ginger and garlic and mix well. Heat the oil in the frying pan, add the prawn mixture and celery and stir-fry for 2-3 minutes. Add the soy sauce, sherry, water and pepper, and bring to the boil. Add the toasted almonds and heat for 30 seconds, stirring.

Garnish with spring onion flowers (see Recipe 96) and serve hot.

96 CRAB IN BLACK BEAN SAUCE

Preparation time:
35 minutes

Cooking time:
12-15 minutes

Serves 4

Calories:
345 per portion

YOU WILL NEED:
2 tablespoons oil
2 tablespoons salted black beans,
  coarsely chopped
2 garlic cloves, crushed
2 tablespoons finely chopped root
  ginger
4 spring onions, chopped
250 g/9 oz lean pork, finely minced
1 large cooked crab, cut into pieces
2 tablespoons dry sherry
300 ml/½ pint chicken stock
2 eggs, beaten
1-2 teaspoons sesame oil
spring onion flowers, to garnish
(see Cook's Tip)

Heat the oil in a wok or large frying pan, add the black beans, garlic, ginger and spring onions and stir-fry briskly for 30 seconds. Add the pork and brown quickly for 1 minute. Add the crab, sherry and stock and boil rapidly for 8-10 minutes.

Combine the eggs and sesame oil and stir into the wok. Stir for 30 seconds, until the egg has cooked into strands. Transfer to a warmed serving dish, garnish with spring onion flowers and serve immediately.

■ COOK'S TIP

Serve a stir-fried vegetable such as Stir-fried Chinese Leaves (recipe 189) with this dish. Noodles or plain boiled rice would also make suitable accompaniments.

■ COOK'S TIP

To make spring onion flowers, trim the green top and remove the white part. Shred the top, leaving 2.5 cm/1 inch attached at the base. Immerse in iced water.

MEAT

A cosmopolitan choice of recipes from many different countries is provided in this chapter. Many of the recipes show how very successfully fruit and meat can be combined. There are plenty of wholesome casseroles for feeding the family as well as more sophisticated dishes for special occasions.

97   CUTLETS WITH TARRAGON

Preparation time:
25 minutes

Cooking time:
25 minutes

Serves 4

Calories:
479 per portion

YOU WILL NEED:
50 g/2 oz butter
2 shallots, very finely chopped
250 g/9 oz button mushrooms, very finely chopped
8 lamb cutlets, trimmed
salt and pepper
150 ml/¼ pint dry white wine
2 tablespoons chopped tarragon
½ teaspoon Dijon mustard
8 artichoke hearts, steamed and sprinkled with lemon juice
tarragon sprigs, to garnish

Melt the butter in a saucepan, add the shallots and cook for 5 minutes. Add the mushrooms, cover and cook for 1 minute. Remove the lid and cook rapidly for 2 minutes; set aside.

Season the cutlets with salt and pepper and brown quickly on both sides in a hot frying pan or wok, then cook for 4 minutes on each side. Remove and keep hot. Add the wine to the pan and stir well. Add half the tarragon and the mustard, bring to the boil and cook rapidly for 5 minutes, until reduced by half. Return the cutlets and heat through.

Arrange the cutlets on a warmed serving dish. Spoon the sauce over the meat and sprinkle with the remaining tarragon. Garnish with the artichoke hearts stuffed with the mushroom mixture and tarragon sprigs. Serve immediately.

98   SKEWERED LAMB

Preparation time:
20 minutes, plus marinating

Cooking time:
10 minutes

Serves 4

Calories:
347 per portion

YOU WILL NEED:
450 g/1 lb lamb fillet, cut into 2.5 cm/ 1 inch cubes
¼ teaspoon crushed black peppercorns
salt
150 ml/¼ pint dry white wine
coarsely grated rind of ½ orange
pinch of ground cinnamon
1 small onion, thinly sliced
FOR THE SAUCE
1 small onion, finely chopped
1 tablespoon olive oil
pinch of saffron strands
1 egg yolk
2 tablespoons natural low-fat yogurt
juice of ½ orange
1 teaspoon cornflour
artificial liquid sweetener, to taste

Put the cubed lamb into a shallow dish with the peppercorns, salt, white wine, orange rind, cinnamon and sliced onion. Cover and chill for 2 hours. Drain the meat, reserving the marinade and thread on to skewers. Grill the kebabs under a preheated grill 4-5 minutes each side.

Meanwhile make the sauce. Fry the chopped onion in the olive oil for 3 minutes. Add the strained marinade and the saffron and bubble briskly for 1 minute. Blend the egg yolk with the yogurt, orange juice and cornflour; add to the sauce and stir over a gentle heat until lightly thickened. Add a little artificial sweetener if necessary.

Serve the cooked kebabs accompanied by the sauce.

99   LAMB WITH APPLE RINGS

Preparation time:
10 minutes, plus
soaking

Cooking time:
20-25 minutes

Serves 4

Calories:
575 per portion

YOU WILL NEED:
8 small noisettes of lamb, trimmed of
  excess fat
2 tablespoons wholemeal flour
freshly ground black pepper
½ teaspoon dried oregano
150 ml/¼ pint chicken stock
1 teaspoon grated orange rind
2 tablespoons orange juice
8 dried apple rings, soaked for 1-2
  hours and drained
salt
sprigs of oregano, to garnish

Dry the lamb and toss it in the flour seasoned with pepper and oregano. Place the noisettes in a non-stick frying pan over a moderate heat and cook for about 3 minutes on each side until they are evenly browned. Reduce the heat and cook them for about 10 minutes, turning them once, until they are cooked the way you like them. Transfer the noisettes to a warmed serving dish and keep them warm. Wipe the frying pan with absorbent kitchen paper to remove any traces of fat.

Add the stock, orange rind, orange juice and apple rings to the pan, season with salt and pepper and bring to the boil. Lower the heat and simmer fo 5 minutes, or until the apple rings are just tender.

Pour the sauce over the lamb, arrange the apple rings and garnish with the oregano.

100 LAMB WITH PIQUANT SAUCE

Preparation time:
15 minutes, plus
marinating

Cooking time:
10-15 minutes

Serves 4

Calories:
349 per portion

YOU WILL NEED:
8 lamb cutlets, trimmed
2 beef stock cubes
8 tablespoons Worcestershire sauce
2 teaspoons chopped fresh rosemary
1 teaspoon ground coriander
120 ml/4 fl oz water
salt and pepper

Put the cutlets in a flameproof dish. Crumble the stock cubes into the Worcestershire sauce and stir in the rosemary and coriander. Pour over the lamb and leave to marinate for at least 3 hours, turning frequently.

Remove the lamb from the marinade and cook under a hot grill for 10 minutes, or until the lamb is cooked to your taste. Turn the meat frequently, spooning over some of the marinade to prevent burning.

Put the remaining marinade in a saucepan with the water, salt and pepper, and bring to the boil. Arrange the lamb cutlets on a heated serving dish and pour the sauce over.

▓ COOK'S TIP

Try using cooking apples,
instead of dried apple rings.
Peel, core and cut into slices
about 5 mm/¼ inch thick.
Cooking time will depend
on the type of apple.

▓ COOK'S TIP

Stock cubes tend to be very
salty, so add the minimum
of salt to the marinade.
Check the contents of the
stock cubes and avoid those
with additives.

101 LAMB RATATOUILLE

Preparation time:	YOU WILL NEED:
25 minutes, plus draining	1 large aubergine, halved lengthways and sliced
	salt and pepper
Cooking time:	1 tablespoon olive oil
1¼ hours	1 kg/2¼ lb boned shoulder of lamb, cubed
Oven temperature:	1 large onion, sliced
180°C, 350°F, gas 4	750 g/1½ lb courgettes, sliced
Serves 6	½ green pepper, seeded and sliced
Calories:	1 × 400 g/14 oz can tomatoes
291 per portion	1 teaspoon dried basil

Sprinkle the aubergine slices with salt and leave to drain for 30 minutes. Rinse and pat the slices dry with absorbent kitchen paper.

Put the lamb cubes in a deep non-stick frying pan over a moderate heat and brown on all sides, then remove and set aside.

Add the onion to the pan with the oil and fry until softened. Add the aubergine, courgettes, red and green peppers, tomatoes with their juice, basil and salt and pepper to taste. Cover and cook for 10 minutes.

Stir the lamb cubes into the vegetable mixture. Cover again and cook in the oven for 1 hour, or until tender.

102 PAPRIKA AND ORANGE LAMB

Preparation time:	YOU WILL NEED:
20 minutes, plus marinating	500 g/1¼ lb lamb fillet, cut into 2.5 cm/1 inch cubes
Cooking time:	1 large red pepper, seeded and cut into 2.5 cm/1 inch pieces
15-20 minutes	FOR THE MARINADE
Oven temperature:	1 tablespoon olive oil
190°C, 375°F, gas 5	2 tablespoons tomato purée
	1 teaspoon paprika
Serves 4	2 tablespoons red wine
Calories:	1 small onion, grated
316 per portion	grated rind and juice of 1 small orange
	2 teaspoons honey
	3 drops Tabasco
	salt and pepper
	FOR THE GARNISH
	4 rosemary sprigs
	4 orange slices

Put the lamb cubes in a shallow dish. Combine the marinade ingredients in a bowl. Pour over the lamb and stir. Cover and refrigerate for 6-8 hours or overnight.

Arrange the lamb on four kebab skewers with the pepper pieces. Place on a rack over a dish or tin and spoon the remaining marinade over the kebabs. Place rosemary sprigs below the kebabs and cook in the oven for 20-30 minutes, or under a preheated medium hot grill for 15-20 minutes, turning once. Put on a heated serving dish, garnish with rosemary sprigs and orange slices.

■ COOK'S TIP

Trim away all the fat from the lamb before cutting it into cubes. Lamb contains quite a lot of invisible fat so it is easy to brown in a dry non-stick pan.

■ COOK'S TIP

Rosemary is an ideal herb to use with lamb. Try adding a couple of sprigs of the herb to the marinade to give the meat a subtle and delicious fragrance. For a more pronounced orange flavour, cut an orange into slices and alternate with the pieces of pepper on the skewer.

103 STIR-FRIED GARLIC LAMB

Preparation time:
15 minutes, plus
marinating

Cooking time:
5 minutes

Serves 4

Calories:
249 per portion

YOU WILL NEED:
350 g/12 oz lamb fillet
2 tablespoons dry sherry
2 tablespoons light soy sauce
1 tablespoon dark soy sauce
1 teaspoon sesame oil
1 tablespoon oil
6 garlic cloves, thinly sliced
1×1-cm/½-inch piece fresh root
  ginger, finely chopped
1 leek, thinly sliced diagonally
4 spring onions, chopped
spring onion flowers, to garnish
(see Recipe 96)

Cut the lamb into thin slices across the grain. Combine the sherry, soy sauces and sesame oil, add the lamb and toss until well coated. Leave to marinate for 15 minutes, then drain, reserving the marinade.

Heat the oil in a non-stick frying pan, add the meat and about 2 teaspoons of the marinade and fry briskly for about 2 minutes, until well browned. Add the garlic, ginger, leek and spring onions and fry for a further 3 minutes.

Transfer to a warmed serving plate, garnish with the spring onion flowers and serve immediately.

104 LAMB CUTLETS PROVENCAL

Preparation time:
20 minutes, plus
marinating

Cooking time:
15 minutes

Serves 4

Calories:
470 per portion

YOU WILL NEED:
8 lamb cutlets, trimmed
2 teaspoons olive oil
3 tablespoons red wine
salt and pepper
1 tablespoon chopped fresh basil
1 red pepper, seeded and chopped
6 tomatoes, peeled, seeded and
  chopped
4 courgettes, chopped
1 small onion, finely chopped
300 ml/½ pint chicken stock
1 garlic clove, crushed
1 tablespoon tomato purée
fresh basil, to garnish

Put the lamb cutlets into a shallow dish with the olive oil, wine, salt and pepper to taste and the chopped basil; cover and chill for 4 hours.

Put the red pepper, tomatoes, courgettes and onion into a saucepan with the chicken stock, garlic, tomato purée and salt and pepper to taste; simmer gently until the vegetables are just tender.

Drain the marinade from the lamb cutlets; blend the marinade and vegetable sauce in a liquidizer until smooth. Cook the lamb cutlets under a preheated grill for 2-3 minutes on each side. Heat the sauce through.

Spoon a pool of vegetable sauce on to four plates and carefully arrange two cutlets on top of each. Garnish with sprigs of basil and serve.

▓ COOK'S TIP

*This recipe originated in the
northern part of China. The
lamb is always cooked in a
wok there but a frying pan
is a satisfactory substitute.*

▓ COOK'S TIP

*If preferred, the sauce can
be served separately in a
sauceboat, rather than
spooned on to each plate.*

105 SOMERSET LAMB CHOPS

Preparation time:
15 minutes

Cooking time:
1¾ hours

Oven temperature:
180°C, 350°F, gas 4

Serves 4

Calories:
466 per portion

YOU WILL NEED:
15 g/½ oz butter
1 large onion, thinly sliced
2 large cooking apples, peeled, cored and sliced
2 tablespoons raisins
salt and pepper
8 lamb chops, trimmed
150 ml/¼ pint dry cider

Melt the butter in a non-stick frying pan. Add the onion and fry until softened. Remove the onion from the pan with a slotted spoon and spread half over the bottom of a casserole. Cover with half the apple slices and sprinkle with half the raisins, and salt and pepper to taste.

Put the chops in the frying pan and brown on both sides. Drain the chops and place in the casserole. Cover with the remaining onion and apples and sprinkle with the remaining raisins, salt and pepper. Pour in the cider. Cover the casserole and cook in the oven for 1½ hours, or until the chops are very tender.

106 PAPRIKA LAMB

Preparation time:
15 minutes, plus marinating

Cooking time:
1¼ hours

Oven temperature:
190°C, 375°F, gas 5

Serves 4

Calories:
233 per portion

YOU WILL NEED:
4 lamb chops, trimmed
1 onion, finely chopped
150 ml/¼ pint natural low-fat yogurt
2 teaspoons paprika
FOR THE MARINADE
2 tablespoons dry white wine
2 teaspoons lemon juice
½ teaspoon sugar
½ teaspoon dried thyme
salt and pepper
FOR THE GARNISH
paprika
parsley sprigs

Mix together the marinade ingredients, with salt and pepper to taste. Place the chops in the marinade and leave for 2-3 hours.

Drain the chops and dry with absorbent kitchen paper. Place them in a shallow ovenproof dish. Sprinkle the onion over the chops and cover with foil. Cook in the oven for 1 hour.

Mix the yogurt with the paprika and spoon over the chops. Continue cooking for a further 15 minutes. Serve sprinkled with paprika and garnished with parsley.

▦ COOK'S TIP

Pork chops, trimmed of fat, can be cooked in exactly the same way. Serve with a crisp green side salad.

▦ COOK'S TIP

This way of cooking lamb chops is based on a typical Hungarian recipe but natural low-fat yogurt is far lower in calories than the traditional soured cream.

For a richer sauce, try combining some smetana with the yogurt.

107 SPINACH-STUFFED LAMB

Preparation time:
20 minutes

Cooking time:
45-55 minutes

Oven temperature:
180°C, 350°F, gas 4

Serves 4

Calories:
174 per portion

YOU WILL NEED:
225 g/8 oz fresh or frozen spinach,
  cooked, drained thoroughly and
  chopped
15 g/½ oz fresh mint, finely chopped
4 garlic cloves, finely chopped
1 teaspoon vinegar
pinch of sugar
salt and pepper
½ small boned leg of lamb (knuckle
  end), about 400 g/ 14 oz
175 ml/6 fl oz red wine
fresh mint sprigs, to garnish

Mix the spinach with the mint, garlic, vinegar, sugar and add salt and pepper to taste.

Trim every scrap of fat off the lamb. Lay it out flat with the boned side up and spread the spinach mixture over. Fold the meat over and secure with string as if tying a parcel. Lay the meat in a roasting dish or pan and pour over the red wine, adding a little water if the pan is much larger than the meat. Cook in the oven for 45-55 minutes, depending on how well done you like lamb.

Transfer to a hot carving platter and cut into thick slices. Pour off the excess fat from the roasting pan and pour the remaining juices over the lamb slices. Serve immediately with rice, garnishing the lamb with fresh mint.

108 SHOULDER OF LAMB STUFFED WITH APRICOTS

Preparation time:
20 minutes, plus
soaking

Cooking time:
1½ hours

Oven temperature:
200°C, 400°F, gas 6

Serves 6

Calories:
431 per portion

YOU WILL NEED:
175 g/6 oz dried apricots
25 g/1 oz chopped onion
2 teaspoons chopped fresh rosemary
  or 1 teaspoon dried rosemary
75 g/3 oz wholemeal breadcrumbs
1 egg, beaten
salt and pepper
1 x 1.5 kg/3 lb shoulder of lamb,
  boned

Soak the apricots overnight. Drain and reserve the soaking liquid.

Roughly chop the apricots, add the onion, rosemary and breadcrumbs. Add the beaten egg to the mixture to bind. Add a little apricot soaking liquid, if necessary, and salt and pepper to taste.

Spoon the stuffing into the lamb bone cavity and sew up the edges, using a trussing needle and string, to enclose the stuffing completely. Roast in the oven for 1½ hours, or until tender.

▌COOK'S TIP

Ask the butcher to remove the bone but do not let him roll the lamb. The piece of meat should be roughly triangular.

▌COOK'S TIP

If any meat remains on a joint after the meal, the joint should be put on a clean plate as the juices sour quickly and would spoil the meat. You could save preparation time by using no-soak dried apricots.

109 ITALIAN VEAL CASSEROLE

Preparation time:
20 minutes

Cooking time:
1¼-1¾ hours

Oven temperature:
180°C, 350°F, gas 4

Serves 2

Calories:
301 per portion

YOU WILL NEED:
1 tablespoon oil
350 g/12 oz lean veal, cubed
1 garlic clove, crushed
1 small onion, sliced
½ green pepper, seeded and chopped
150 g/5 oz tomatoes, peeled and chopped
200 ml/7 fl oz light stock
salt and pepper
bouquet garni
chopped parsley, to garnish

Heat the oil in a frying pan, add the veal and fry, turning, until golden brown all over. Add the garlic and onion and cook until they are soft.

Stir in the green pepper, tomatoes, stock and salt and pepper to taste. Transfer to a 1.2 litre/2 pint casserole. Add the bouquet garni. Cover and cook in the oven for 1¼-1½ hours.

Remove the bouquet garni and skim off any excess fat. Serve hot, garnished with parsley.

110 VEAL PAPRIKA

Preparation time:
10 minutes

Cooking time:
10 minutes

Serves 4

Calories:
251 per portion

YOU WILL NEED:
4 veal fillets, about 175 g/6 oz each
1 tablespoon lemon juice
4 tablespoons tomato purée
3 teaspoons paprika
300 ml/½ pint natural low-fat yogurt
salt and pepper

Put the veal fillets on the rack of a grill pan. Cook under a fairly hot grill for about 5 minutes on each side (depending on the thickness of the fillets), spooning over some of the lemon juice to prevent the meat burning.

Mix together the tomato purée, paprika and remaining lemon juice and heat gently. Remove from the heat and stir in the yogurt and salt and pepper to taste.

Put the veal fillets on a warmed serving plate and pour the sauce over.

COOK'S TIP

A classic bouquet garni consists of parsley stalks, bay leaves and thyme sprigs. There is much more flavour in the parsley stalks than in the decorative leaves.

COOK'S TIP

This sauce has a rather sharp taste. If you prefer a slightly sweeter sauce, use fresh orange juice instead of the lemon juice. Alternatively, you could add a few drops of artifical liquid sweetener just before serving.

111 HUNGARIAN VEAL

Preparation time:
20 minutes

Cooking time:
1¼-1¾ hours

Oven temperature:
180°C, 350°F, gas 4

Serves 4

Calories:
226 per portion

YOU WILL NEED:
1 tablespoon oil
500 g/1¼ lb lean veal, cut into cubes
1 onion, sliced
3 teaspoons paprika
1 green pepper, seeded and chopped
50 g/2 oz button mushrooms, sliced
300 ml/½ pint tomato juice
85 ml/3 fl oz beef stock
½ teaspoon sugar
salt and pepper
grated nutmeg
1 bay leaf
4 tablespoons natural low-fat yogurt
chopped parsley, to garnish

Heat the oil in a large frying pan, add the veal and fry for 5 minutes. Add the onion and fry for 2-3 minutes. Stir in the paprika and cook for 1 minute. Add the green pepper, mushrooms, tomato juice, stock, sugar, salt, pepper and nutmeg to taste, and the bay leaf. Bring to the boil, stirring, then transfer to a 1.75 litre/3 pint casserole.

Cook in the oven for 1-1½ hours. Stir in the yogurt just before serving. Garnish with chopped parsley.

112 VEAL PÖRKÖLT

Preparation time:
15 minutes

Cooking time:
1 hour

Serves 6

Calories:
457 per portion

YOU WILL NEED:
750 g/1½ lb pie veal in one piece
25 g/1 oz pure lard
2 large onions, finely chopped
1 tablespoon sweet paprika
½ teaspoon salt
1 tablespoon water
1 green pepper, halved and seeded
1 large tomato, halved
450 g/1 lb pasta shells or noodles, cooked

Cut the meat into large pieces of about 5 cm/2 inches.

Heat the lard in a heavy-based saucepan and fry the onions until golden. Take the pan off the heat and add the paprika, stir thoroughly, then add the meat and return to a gentle heat. Stir and add the salt and the water. Cover and simmer slowly, stirring from time to time and adding a little more water should it look at all dry. After 30 minutes add the halved green pepper and tomato, cover and continue cooking until the meat is really tender; the longer and slower the better.

Just before serving, remove the green pepper, chop up and combine with the veal. Turn the pörkölt into a large warmed serving dish and surround with pasta shells or noodles.

■ COOK'S TIP

For an authentic flavour, use genuine rose paprika. This popular spice is obtainable from some Middle European delicatessens in several *different strengths, depending on which portion of the capsicum pod was used.*

■ COOK'S TIP

A boned knuckle of veal is the ideal joint for this Hungarian dish. 1-2 tablespoons of olive oil may be substituted for the lard to fry the onions.

113 VEAL WITH OLIVES

Preparation time:
15 minutes

Cooking time:
30-35 minutes

Serves 4

Calories:
305 per portion

YOU WILL NEED:
1 tablespoon olive oil
4 veal noisettes, trimmed of fat, about
    150 g/5 oz each
1 small onion, thinly sliced
1 bay leaf
1 strip of lemon rind
300 ml/½ pint dry white wine
50 g/2 oz green olives, stoned and
    finely chopped
1 teaspoon fresh thyme
salt and pepper
3 tablespoons natural low-fat yogurt
1 egg yolk
FOR THE GARNISH
8 large green olives
sprigs of fresh thyme

Heat the olive oil in a non-stick frying pan and gently fry the noisettes until lightly golden. Add the onion, bay leaf, lemon rind, white wine, stoned green olives and thyme with salt and pepper to taste. Cover and simmer for 25 minutes, until tender. Remove and keep warm.

Discard the bay leaf and blend the cooking liquid with the yogurt and egg yolk. Heat the sauce through very gently without allowing it to come to the boil.

Spoon the hot sauce over the veal and garnish with the olives and sprigs of thyme.

114 SAUTE DE VEAU MARENGO

Preparation time:
30 minutes

Cooking time:
2¼ hours

Oven temperature:
160°C, 325°F, gas 3

Serves 6

Calories:
309 per portion

YOU WILL NEED:
1 kg/2¼ lb lean stewing veal
wholemeal flour for coating
salt and pepper
1 tablespoon oil
2 onions, chopped
6 tablespoons dry white vermouth
300 ml/½ pint dry white wine
500 g/1 ¼ lb tomatoes, peeled, seeded
    and chopped
2 tablespoons tomato purée
1 teaspoon chopped basil
1 teaspoon chopped oregano
strip of orange rind
2 garlic cloves, crushed
250 g/9 oz button mushrooms
chopped basil, to garnish (optional)

Cut the veal into 2.5 cm/1 inch cubes. Season the flour with salt and pepper and use to coat the veal lightly.

Heat the oil in a non-stick frying pan, add the veal and fry until browned on all sides. Transfer to a flameproof casserole. Add the onion to the pan and fry until golden. Add to the casserole, with the remaining ingredients. Bring to the boil, then cook in the oven for about 2 hours, until tender. Remove the orange rind.

Garnish with basil, if using.

▧ COOK'S TIP

*Pare the lemon carefully to
ensure no pith is attached to
the rind. If you use olives
that have been preserved in
brine, rinse thoroughly in
cold water.*

▧ COOK'S TIP

*For a more economical
version of this dish, replace
the white wine with chicken
or veal stock. The dry white
vermouth gives a distinctive
flavour. Serve with noodles.*

115 VEAL PAUPIETTES

Preparation time:
20 minutes

Cooking time:
20-25 minutes

Serves 4

Calories:
293 per portion

YOU WILL NEED:
4 veal escalopes, flattened, about
    150 g/5 oz each
1 teaspoon grated lemon rind
1 small onion, chopped
freshly ground black pepper
1 tablespoon chopped sage
4 large lettuce leaves
20 g/¾ oz butter
1 tablespoon olive oil
150 ml/¼ pint dry white wine
150 ml/¼ pint chicken stock
2 parsnips, peeled, chopped and
    cooked
2 tablespoons natural low-fat yogurt
2 canned red pimentos
1 tablespoon chopped chives
salt

Sprinkle the escalopes with the lemon rind, onion, pepper and sage. Lay a lettuce leaf on top of each and roll up. Tie neatly with fine string.

Heat the butter and oil in a shallow pan; add the prepared veal paupiettes and cook until evenly coloured on all sides. Add the wine and chicken stock; cover and simmer until the veal is tender.

Meanwhile, blend the parsnips, yogurt and red pimentos in a liquidizer. Mix in the chives and season. Heat through in a double saucepan.

Spoon the purée on to a warmed serving dish and arrange the paupiettes on top.

▓ COOK'S TIP

Use a heavy metal cleaver to flatten the veal escalopes. If you dip the cleaver in cold water first, this will help to prevent your tearing the veal.

116 VEAL WITH ORANGE

Preparation time:
25 minutes

Cooking time:
1¾-2¼ hours

Oven temperature:
180°C, 350°F, gas 4

Serves 4

Calories:
304 per portion

YOU WILL NEED:
1 tablespoon oil
750 g/1½ lb lean pie veal, cubed
1 onion, sliced
3 tablespoons wholemeal flour
300 ml/½ pint chicken stock
150 ml/¼ pint unsweetened orange
    juice
salt and pepper
2 oranges, peeled and sliced
watercress, to garnish

Heat the oil in a non-stick frying pan. Add the veal cubes and brown on all sides. Transfer with a slotted spoon to a casserole. Add the onion to the pan and fry until golden brown. Add to the casserole.

Stir the flour into the fat remaining in the pan and cook for 3 minutes. Gradually stir in the stock and orange juice and bring to the boil. Season with salt and pepper to taste. Pour over the veal cubes. Arrange the orange slices, overlapping, on top.

Cook in the oven for 1½-2 hours, or until the veal is tender. Garnish with watercress.

▓ COOK'S TIP

Depending on the time of year different varieties of oranges are available. The best types to use in casseroles are those with thin skins, juicy flesh and few pips, such as the Navel and Valencia.

117 BEEF WITH PLUMS

Preparation time:
20 minutes

Cooking time:
10 minutes

Serves 2

Calories:
315 per portion

YOU WILL NEED:
1 tablespoon oil
1 onion, thinly sliced
1 garlic clove, crushed
2-3 pieces beef for beef olives, cut into thin slivers
2-3 dessert plums, stoned and cut into slices
2-3 mushrooms, thinly sliced
1 tablespoon sherry
1 tablespoon soy sauce
2 teaspoons cornflour, blended with 2 tablespoons water
chopped spring onion tops, to garnish

Heat the oil in a large frying pan, add the onion and fry for 2 minutes. Stir in the garlic, then push the mixture to one side of the pan. Tilt the pan to let the juices run out of the onion and over the base. Scatter in the meat strips and stir-fry over a high heat for 2 minutes, until the meat is evenly coloured.

Lower the heat and add the plums and mushrooms. Continue to stir-fry for 1 minute, then stir in the sherry, soy sauce and blended cornflour. Cook, stirring, until the sauce has thickened.

Garnish with spring onions and serve with wholemeal tagliatelle and green vegetables.

118 CHILLI BEEF

Preparation time:
20 minutes

Cooking time:
30-35 minutes

Serves 4

Calories:
380 per portion

YOU WILL NEED:
1 tablespoon olive oil
1 small onion, finely chopped
1 garlic clove, crushed
450 g/1 lb lean minced beef
1 tablespoon chilli powder
1 tablespoon tomato purée
300 ml/½ pint beef stock
6 tomatoes, peeled, seeded and chopped
1 small red pepper, seeded and chopped
1 x 225 g/8 oz can kidney beans, rinsed and drained
FOR THE GARNISH
4 tablespoons natural low-fat yogurt
chilli powder (optional)

Heat the oil and fry the onion gently for 3 minutes; add the garlic and beef and fry until browned. Stir in the chilli powder and cook for 1 minute. Add the tomato purée, beef stock, tomatoes, chopped red pepper and kidney beans. Cover and simmer gently for 20-25 minutes, until the minced beef is tender.

Spoon the minced beef on to warmed plates and place a tablespoon of yogurt next to it. Sprinkle a little chilli powder over the yogurt, if liked. Serve immediately with rice or a salad.

■ COOK'S TIP

The beef used for beef olives is sold rolled up in thin raw slices. Imported plums are often on sale outside the short home season.

■ COOK'S TIP

If you have not used chilli powder before, it is best to add only 1 teaspoon at first as you may find that 1 tablespoon makes the beef too fiery.

119 STIR-FRIED BEEF WITH PEPPERS

Preparation time:
15 minutes

Cooking time:
10-12 minutes

Serves 4

Calories:
252 per portion

YOU WILL NEED:
1 tablespoon olive oil
1 onion, thinly sliced
1 large garlic clove, cut into thin strips
450 g/1 lb fillet steak, cut into thin strips
1 red pepper, seeded and cut into matchstick strips
1 green pepper, seeded and cut into matchstick strips
1 tablespoon soy sauce
2 tablespoons dry sherry
salt and pepper
1 tablespoon chopped fresh rosemary

Heat the olive oil in a deep frying pan or wok and stir-fry the onion and garlic for 2 minutes. Add the strips of beef and stir-fry briskly until evenly browned on all sides and almost tender. Add the strips of red and green pepper and stir-fry for a further 2 minutes. Add the soy sauce, sherry, salt and pepper to taste and the rosemary, and stir-fry for a further 1-2 minutes.

Serve piping hot with brown rice.

120 SUMMER VEGETABLE HOTPOT

Preparation time:
20 minutes

Cooking time:
35 minutes

Oven temperature:
200°C, 400°F, gas 6

Serves 4

Calories:
346 per portion

YOU WILL NEED:
450 g/1 lb lean minced beef
1 teaspoon coriander seeds
½ teaspoon very coarsely ground black pepper
½ teaspoon cumin seeds
½ teaspoon salt
1 tablespoon red wine vinegar
2 teaspoons oil
3 x 400 g/14 oz cans tomatoes
1 bay leaf
1 dried chilli
1 kg/2¼ lb French beans, chopped into 2 cm/¾ inch lengths
1 tablespoon red wine

Put the minced beef in a bowl and add the coriander, black pepper, cumin seeds, salt and vinegar. Oil your hands lightly and knead the mixture for a minute before forming walnut-sized balls.

Heat the oil in a frying pan and seal the meatballs. Put in a casserole and add the tomatoes, bay leaf and chilli.

Cook in the oven for about 5 minutes, then add the French beans and red wine. Cook, uncovered, for 15-25 minutes, until the beans are just tender.

COOK'S TIP

Fillet steak is the most suitable cut to use for this dish. Less expensive cuts tend to be tougher and are better suited to slower methods of cooking. You *can sometimes buy fillet steak at a reduced price late on a Saturday.*

COOK'S TIP

This hotpot can be cooked on a barbecue. Carefully embed the casserole in the hot coal and allow to heat up before adding the oil.

121 MEATBALLS IN TOMATO SAUCE

Preparation time:
15 minutes

Cooking time:
45-50 minutes

Serves 4

Calories:
349 per portion

YOU WILL NEED:
500 g/1¼ lb lean minced beef
1 garlic clove, crushed
1 tablespoon chopped parsley
½ teaspoon cumin seeds (optional)
salt and pepper
1 egg, beaten
chopped parsley, to garnish
FOR THE SAUCE
2 onions, finely chopped
1 x 400 g/14 oz can tomatoes
1 tablespoon tomato purée
½ teaspoon sugar
grated nutmeg

Put the beef, garlic, parsley, cumin seeds (if using) and salt and pepper to taste in a bowl; mix well. Bind the mixture with the egg, then divide into 20 and shape into balls on a floured surface.

Place the sauce ingredients, with nutmeg, salt and pepper to taste, in a large flameproof casserole. Bring to the boil, then lower the heat. Carefully place the meatballs in the liquid, cover and simmer gently for 40-45 minutes, stirring occasionally.

Transfer the meatballs to a warmed serving dish and pour the sauce over. Serve garnished with chopped parsley.

122 STEAK WITH VEGETABLES

Preparation time:
20 minutes

Cooking time:
13-15 minutes

Serves 4

Calories:
397 per portion

YOU WILL NEED:
4 grilling steaks, about 175 g/6 oz each
1 tablespoon oil
1 onion, thinly sliced
1 carrot, thinly sliced
2 potatoes, thinly sliced
2 celery sticks, sliced
4-6 spring cabbage or spinach leaves, shredded
50 g/2 oz small broccoli or cauliflower florets
50 g/2 oz mushrooms, sliced
¼ cucumber, sliced
2-3 tomatoes, cut into wedges
2 tablespoons soy sauce

Cook the steak under a preheated hot grill for 3-5 minutes on each side, depending on thickness and personal taste.

Heat the oil in a large non-stick frying pan, add the onion and fry for 2 minutes. Add the carrot, potato and about 4 tablespoons hot water and stir-fry over a high heat for 3 minutes, using two large wooden spoons to turn the vegetables. Add the celery, cabbage or spinach, and broccoli or cauliflower, and stir-fry for 2 minutes, adding a little more water if necessary to prevent sticking. Add the mushrooms, cucumber and tomatoes and stir-fry for another minute. Add the soy sauce and stir well. The vegetables should be tender but still crisp, with a rich gravy in the bottom of the pan. Serve hot with the steak on warmed plates.

■ COOK'S TIP

If you dip your fingers in cold water when shaping meatballs, this will help to prevent them becoming sticky and the meat mixture crumbling.

■ COOK'S TIP

Stir-fried vegetables are quick, easy and healthy eating. Always start with an onion, then add any root vegetables and green leaves. Add the softest vegetable last. The vegetable juices will combine to make a nutritious sauce.

123 GULYAS

Preparation time:
35 minutes

Cooking time:
1 hour

Serves 8

Calories:
427 per portion

YOU WILL NEED:
25 g/1 oz lard
2 large onions, finely chopped
5 teaspoons sweet paprika
1.25 kg/2¾ lb flank steak, cubed
750 g/1½ lb potatoes
1 teaspoon caraway seeds
2 tablespoons tomato purée
2.25 litres/4 pints chicken stock
3 green peppers, seeded, sliced
salt and pepper
175 g/6 oz plain flour
1 egg, lightly beaten

Heat the lard and fry the onions until well coloured. Remove from the heat and add the paprika. Stir well and add the beef, one of the potatoes peeled and grated, and the caraway seeds. Stir and return to the heat, cover and simmer for 10-15 minutes, stirring from time to time.

Add the tomato purée and a cupful of the stock. Cover and simmer until the meat is nearly done. Add the remaining stock. Peel and cube the remaining potatoes and add them with the green peppers as soon as the soup has come to the boil. Cook until the potatoes are done and the meat is tender. Add salt and pepper to taste.

To make the dumplings: sieve the flour on to a board, make a well in the centre and add the egg and the salt. Work the mixture into a stiff dough adding a drop or two of water, if necessary. Flatten the dough between the palms of your hands. Pinch off pieces the size of kidney beans and add them to the gulyas 10 minutes before serving.

■ COOK'S TIP

If you have a cast-iron cauldron, you can cook this gulyas (pronounced ghoulash) over a bonfire like the Hungarian vagabonds once did.

124 FLEMISH BEEF

Preparation time:
20 minutes

Cooking time:
1¾-2 hours

Oven temperature:
180°C, 350°F, gas 4

Serves 4

Calories:
296 per portion

YOU WILL NEED:
500 g/1¼ lb lean chuck steak, cubed
1 onion, sliced
1 carrot, sliced
1 garlic clove, crushed
75 g/3 oz mushrooms, sliced
300 ml/½ pint light ale
1 beef stock cube
1 teaspoon vinegar
1 teaspoon brown sugar
grated nutmeg
salt and pepper
1 bay leaf
2 teaspoons cornflour
3 tablespoons water
chopped parsley, to garnish

Brown the steak in a non-stick frying pan and place in a 1.75 litre/3 pint casserole. Add the onion, carrot, garlic and mushrooms.

Blend the light ale with the stock cube, vinegar, brown sugar, and nutmeg, salt and pepper to taste. Pour over the meat and vegetables. Add the bay leaf. Cover and cook in the oven for 1½ hours, or until the meat is tender.

Mix the cornflour with the water and stir into the casserole. Cook for 15-20 minutes. Serve garnished with chopped parsley.

■ COOK'S TIP

When you are making a dish such as a casserole that needs a long cooking time, economize on fuel by using the oven to cook another dish at the same time.

125 BEEF WITH ORANGE

Preparation time:
20 minutes

Cooking time:
1¼-1½ hours

Oven temperature:
160°C, 325°F, gas 3

Serves 4

Calories:
155 per portion

YOU WILL NEED:
5 teaspoons plain wholemeal flour
salt and pepper
350 g/12 oz lean chuck steak, cubed
15 g/½ oz butter
1 small onion, chopped
½ green pepper, seeded and chopped
grated rind and juice of 2 small
    oranges
200 ml/7 fl oz beef stock
chopped parsley, to garnish

Season the flour with salt and pepper and use to coat the meat. Melt the butter in a non-stick frying pan, add the onion and pepper and fry until soft. Add the meat and fry, turning, until evenly browned. Transfer to a 900 ml/ 1½ pint casserole.

Stir in the orange rind and juice, stock and salt and pepper to taste. Cover and cook in the oven for 1-1¼ hours. Serve hot, garnished with parsley.

126 BEEF AND ARTICHOKES

Preparation time:
25 minutes, plus marinating

Cooking time:
1¼ hours

Serves 6

Calories:
259 per portion

YOU WILL NEED:
1 kg/2¼ lb lean chuck steak, cut into
    cubes
½ teaspoon allspice
½ teaspoon ground cinnamon
½ teaspoon salt
coarsely ground black pepper
4 garlic cloves
8 tablespoons red wine
1 tablespoon oil
½ teaspoon ground cumin
750 g/1½ lb Jerusalem artichokes,
    blanched and scraped, cut into
    chunks

Put the meat in a bowl and sprinkle over the allspice, cinnamon, salt and pepper. Add 2 of the garlic cloves, chopped. Pour over the wine and mix well. Cover and leave to marinate for at least 4 hours (not more than 24).

Heat the oil and fry the remaining garlic, halved, with the cumin. Strain the meat and add to the pan, reserving the marinade. Seal the meat over a high heat, then transfer to a flameproof casserole. Add the artichokes and marinade, cover and simmer for 1 hour.

▨ COOK'S TIP

Nothing really compares with the flavour of home-made stock – simmered slowly until it is well reduced and sets in a thick jelly.

▨ COOK'S TIP

The gnarled shapes of Jerusalem artichokes make them rather fiddly to prepare. A potato peeler can be used on the larger artichokes but it is not essential to take the skin off the smaller ones, provided you have scrubbed them thoroughly to remove any traces of earth.

127 PORK AND PRUNES

Preparation time:
10 minutes, plus
soaking

Cooking time:
1¼ hours

Oven temperature:
220°C, 425°F, gas
7; then
160°C, 325°F, gas 3

Serves 4

Calories:
192 per portion

YOU WILL NEED:
20 prunes, soaked overnight in water
4 pork chops, about 175 g/6 oz each,
  trimmed
1 chicken stock cube, crumbled
salt and pepper
1 teaspoon mustard powder
1 tablespoon wine vinegar
parsley sprigs, to garnish

Arrange the prunes in an ovenproof dish. Lay the pork chops on top of the prunes. Add all the remaining ingredients and enough of the prune soaking liquid to cover.

Cook in the oven for 15 minutes, then reduce the temperature and cook for about 1 hour more, or until the chops are tender. Garnish with parsley and serve.

128 COUNTRY PORK CASSEROLE

Preparation time:
20 minutes

Cooking time:
1¼ hours

Oven temperature:
180°C, 350°F, gas 4

Serves 4

Calories:
262 per portion

YOU WILL NEED:
450 g/1 lb pork fillet
25 g/1 oz flour
salt and pepper
2 tablespoons oil
2 onions, sliced
1-2 leeks, sliced
1-3 celery sticks, diced
1 small green pepper, seeded and diced
225 g/8 oz tomatoes, roughly chopped
1 tablespoon lemon juice or white
  wine vinegar
150 ml/¼ pint chicken stock
1-2 tablespoons tomato purée

Cut the pork into neat slices. Blend the flour, salt and pepper and use to coat the meat lightly. Heat the oil in a large non-stick frying pan, fry the pork slices on either side until golden brown and transfer to a casserole. Add the onions, leeks and celery to the pan and fry gently for 10 minutes; do not allow the vegetables to brown. Spoon these vegetables over the pork then add the pepper and tomatoes.

Pour the lemon juice or vinegar, chicken stock and tomato purée into the pan; stir well to absorb any meat juices, season to taste, then spoon over the pork and vegetables. Cover the casserole and cook in the oven for 40-50 minutes, or until the meat is tender.

▨ COOK'S TIP

Serve this quick-to-prepare casserole with steamed sliced courgettes and plain boiled rice. Rinse the prunes in cold water before leaving them to soak overnight to *remove any fragments of leaf.*

▨ COOK'S TIP

The fillet is the leanest cut of pork and also the most tender – it is sometimes called tenderloin. For this dish it is not necessary to buy the fillet in one piece.

129 COTES DE PORC VALLEE D'AUGE

Preparation time: 10 minutes	**YOU WILL NEED:** 4 shallots, chopped
Cooking time: 30 minutes	2 tablespoons chopped parsley salt and pepper 4 pork chops, trimmed
Serves 4	15 g/½ oz butter, melted 150 ml/¼ pint dry cider
Calories: 207 per portion	sage leaves, to garnish

Mix the shallots and parsley together, with salt and pepper to taste. Score the chops on both sides and spread with the mixture. Spoon over a little melted butter. Cook under a preheated medium grill for about 15 minutes on each side until tender.

Transfer the chops to a frying pan. Drain off any excess fat from the grill pan and pour the juices over the chops. Add the cider and boil for 2 minutes until the liquor has reduced.

Transfer to a warmed serving dish and garnish the chops with sage.

130 PORC FARCI AUX PRUNEAUX

Preparation time: 15 minutes, plus soaking	**YOU WILL NEED:** 1.5 kg/3 lb piece pork fillet salt and pepper
Cooking time: 1¾ hours	175 g/6 oz large prunes 25 g/1 oz seedless raisins ½ teaspoon ground mixed spice
Oven temperature: 190°C, 375°F, gas 5	1 tablespoon chopped sage 300 ml/½ pint dry white wine
Serves 6	1 tablespoon redcurrant jelly 150 ml/¼ pint natural low-fat yogurt
Calories: 388 per portion	parsley sprigs, to garnish

Season the pork with salt and pepper and lay flat. Soak the prunes and raisins in boiling water for 30 minutes. Drain well and stone the prunes.

Mix the spice and sage with the prunes and raisins. Spread over the meat, leaving a 2.5 cm/1 inch border. Roll up and secure with string. Place in a roasting pan and pour over half the wine. Cook in the oven for 1½ hours, or until tender.

Transfer to a warmed serving dish. Add the remaining wine to the roasting pan, place over a low heat and bring to the boil. Simmer for 3-4 minutes until reduced to 150 ml/¼ pint. Add the redcurrant jelly and yogurt, check the seasoning and simmer until thickened.

Garnish the meat with parsley. Serve with steamed courgettes and the sauce.

■ COOK'S TIP

The authentic flavour of this classic French dish calls for shallots rather than onions. In Normandy a tablespoon of Calvados is added just before serving.

■ COOK'S TIP

Natural low-fat yogurt has been substituted for the double cream used in the traditional version of this French recipe: the sauce is far less fattening.

131 PORK CASSEROLE WITH FRUIT

Preparation time:
10 minutes

Cooking time:
1¼ hours

Oven temperature:
180°C, 350°F, gas 4

Serves 4

Calories:
284 per portion

YOU WILL NEED:
4 pork chops
1 x 400 g/14 oz can apricot halves in natural juice
1 x 225 g/8 oz can pineapple rings in natural juice
8 prunes, stoned and chopped
5 tablespoons chicken stock
150 ml/¼ pint natural low-fat yogurt
salt and pepper

Put the chops in a frying pan and brown on both sides. Remove the chops from the pan, drain, then arrange in a flameproof casserole.

Drain the apricot halves and pineapple rings, reserving the juice. Place the fruit, with the prunes, on top of the chops to cover them. Mix the stock with 5 tablespoons each of the apricot and pineapple juices. Pour into the casserole. Cover tightly and cook in the oven for about 1 hour or until the chops are tender.

Transfer the chops to a warmed serving dish, being careful not to dislodge the fruit on top. Keep hot.

Boil the liquid in the casserole until reduced to about 150 ml/¼ pint. Skim off any fat, then stir in the yogurt with salt and pepper to taste. Heat through gently and serve this sauce with the pork.

132 PORK WITH PRUNE SAUCE

Preparation time:
15 minutes

Cooking time:
20 minutes

Serves 4

Calories:
316 per portion

YOU WILL NEED:
4 pork loin chops, trimmed
1 tablespoon oil
1 small onion, thinly sliced
1 garlic clove, crushed
1 x 400 g/14 oz can prunes in natural juice
2 teaspoons cornflour
1 tablespoon soy sauce
2 teaspoons wine vinegar
watercress sprigs, to garnish

Cook the pork under a preheated moderate grill for about 10 minutes on each side, or until cooked through.

Meanwhile, heat the oil in a non-stick frying pan, add the onion and fry for 2 minutes, stirring. Stir in the garlic and set aside.

Drain the prunes, reserving the juice. Remove the stones and set aside 4 prunes for garnish. Put the remaining prunes and the juice in a blender or food processor. Add the cornflour, soy sauce, vinegar and onion mixture and work until smooth. Pour into the pan and cook, stirring, until thick and shiny.

Divide the sauce between warmed individual serving plates and lay a grilled pork chop on each one. Garnish with a prune and a watercress sprig.

■ COOK'S TIP

Ideally, let the reduced liquid go cold before skimming off the fat as it is much easier to do then. Alternatively, use absorbent kitchen paper to mop it up.

■ COOK'S TIP

In this recipe canned prunes in natural juice are used but you can replace these with prunes which have been cooked with water until just tender.

133 CHINESE PORK WITH BAMBOO SHOOTS

Preparation time:
15 minutes

Cooking time:
20-25 minutes

Serves 4

Calories:
203 per portion

YOU WILL NEED:
2 tablespoons groundnut oil
300 g/11 oz lean pork, shredded
salt and pepper
1 small Chinese cabbage, shredded
1 tablespoon coarsely chopped
    hazelnuts
1×225 g/8 oz can bamboo shoots,
    drained with juices reserved, and
    sliced
2 tablespoons soy sauce
1 teaspoon curry powder
pinch of chilli powder
small pinch of sugar

Heat the oil in a non-stick frying pan or wok, add the pork and stir-fry quickly until lightly browned. Season with salt and pepper to taste. Add the cabbage, hazelnuts and a few tablespoons of the liquid from the can of bamboo shoots. Cook, stirring, for about 5 minutes.

Add the bamboo shoots, soy sauce, curry powder, chilli powder and sugar, mixing well. Cook gently for a further 10 minutes. Serve immediately.

134 BLACK BEAN CASSEROLE

Preparation time:
20 minutes, plus
soaking

Cooking time:
2½-3 hours

Oven temperature:
180°C, 350°F, gas 4

Serves 4

Calories:
512 per portion

YOU WILL NEED:
400 g/14 oz black beans, soaked
    overnight
1 tablespoon olive oil
2 onions, sliced
2 celery sticks, sliced
2 carrots, sliced
2 garlic cloves, crushed
175 g/6 oz frankfurter sausages, sliced
1 tablespoon tomato purée
1 bay leaf
500 g/1¼ lb tomatoes, peeled and
    chopped
salt and pepper
chopped parsley, to garnish

Drain the beans, put in a pan and cover with cold water. Bring to the boil, boil for 10 minutes, then simmer gently for 1 hour. Drain and reserve 450 ml/¾ pint of the liquid.

Heat the oil in a flameproof casserole, add the onions and fry for 5-10 minutes until transparent. Add the celery, carrots and garlic and fry for 3-4 minutes.

Add the remaining ingredients, with the beans, reserved liquid, and salt and pepper to taste. Cover and cook in the oven for 1-1½ hours until the beans are soft. Sprinkle with the parsley and serve immediately.

COOK'S TIP

Bamboo shoots are a popular ingredient in Chinese vegetable dishes. In China raw shoots are used but the canned variety is used elsewhere.

COOK'S TIP

It is essential that the black beans are soaked overnight and then cooked exactly as described above. Cook a larger quantity and use the surplus in a salad.

135 GREEK VINE LEAVES WITH SAVOURY STUFFING

Preparation time:
15 minutes

Cooking time:
30 minutes

Serves 4

Calories:
222 per portion

YOU WILL NEED:
1 x 425 g/15 oz can vine leaves
2 tablespoons olive oil
150 g/5 oz lean minced beef
1 large onion, finely chopped
¼ fennel bulb, grated
2 garlic cloves, crushed
150 g/5 oz cooked long-grain rice
1 tablespoon chopped dill
1 teaspoon dried oregano
salt and pepper
150 ml/¼ pint dry red wine
150 ml/¼ pint water
4 tablespoons lemon juice

Put the vine leaves in a sieve, rinse and drain thoroughly.

Heat 1 tablespoon of the oil in a large non-stick frying pan. Add the minced meat, onion, fennel and garlic and fry, stirring, until cooked for about 8-10 minutes. Stir in the rice, dill, oregano and salt and pepper to taste. Spread the mixture evenly over the vine leaves. Fold the long sides of the vine leaves over and roll up securely from the shorter edge to make neat parcels.

Mix the remaining oil, the red wine and water in a saucepan, add the stuffed vine leaves, cover and cook over a gentle heat for about 20 minutes. Remove with a slotted spoon to serve.

136 STUFFED CABBAGE

Preparation time:
20 minutes

Cooking time:
2 hours

Oven temperature:
190°C, 375°F, gas 5

Serves 8

Calories:
70 per portion

YOU WILL NEED:
1 medium cabbage
1 tablespoon olive oil
4 back bacon rashers, derinded and chopped
1 onion, chopped
1 garlic clove, crushed
1 egg, beaten
2 tablespoons grated Parmesan cheese
3 tablespoons chopped parsley
salt and pepper
250 ml/8 fl oz chicken stock

Cook the whole cabbage in boiling water for 15 minutes. Drain and cool under cold running water. Cut out the core, then remove the inner cabbage leaves, leaving the outside leaves intact. Chop the inner leaves.

Heat the oil in a non-stick frying pan, add the bacon, chopped cabbage leaves, onion and garlic and fry until the onion is softened. Remove from the heat. Mix together the egg, cheese, parsley and salt and pepper to taste and stir into the cabbage mixture.

Place the cabbage 'shell' of large outside leaves in a casserole lined with foil and fill the shell with the fried mixture. Pour over the stock. Cover and cook in the oven for 1 hour. Uncover the casserole and cook for a further 30 minutes. To serve, lift the cabbage out, then remove the foil.

■ COOK'S TIP

Fresh vine leaves can be used if they are first blanched in boiling water for 2 minutes, then drained and rinsed in cold water. Remove any stalks.

■ COOK'S TIP

Try varying the ingredients of the stuffing by using lean minced beef or chicken dice instead of the bacon. You can omit the Parmesan cheese and use some concentrated tomato purée as a flavouring.

137 LIVER AND BACON HOTPOT

Preparation time:
15 minutes

Cooking time:
1½ hours

Oven temperature:
180°C, 350°F, gas 4

Serves 4

Calories:
519 per portion

YOU WILL NEED:
1 large onion, sliced
2 cooking apples, peeled, cored and
   sliced
150 g/5 oz mushrooms, sliced
200 g/7 oz unsmoked back bacon
   rashers, derinded
750 g/1 ½ lb lamb's liver, sliced
salt and pepper
½ x 400 g/14 oz can consommé
1 x 400 g/14 oz can tomatoes, drained
   and chopped
chopped parsley, to garnish

Spread one-third of the onion over the bottom of a casserole.
Add one-third of the apple slices, then one-third of the mushrooms and bacon, then half the liver. Season well. Continue
making layers in this way. Pour in the consommé and spread
the tomatoes over the top.

Cover tightly and cook in the oven for 1½ hours. Serve garnished with chopped parsley.

138 STIR-FRIED LIVER AND FENNEL

Preparation time:
15 minutes

Cooking time:
12-15 minutes

Serves 6

Calories:
274 per portion

YOU WILL NEED:
750 g/1½ lb calves' liver, trimmed
1 tablespoon oil
1 large fennel bulb, finely sliced into
   thin strips
3 garlic cloves, chopped
3 tablespoons tomato purée
3 tablespoons red wine
salt and pepper
1 tablespoon chopped parsley

Cut the liver into 1 cm/1½ inch-wide strips.

Heat the oil in a heavy frying pan or a wok and add the fennel and garlic. Stir and cook for a few minutes over a medium
to high heat. As soon as the fennel begins to colour slightly,
add the liver and stir continuously. After 1 minute add the
tomato purée and wine, bring to boiling point, simmer for 2
minutes, then remove from the heat. Add salt and pepper to
taste and stir in the parsley.

Serve with rice or steamed potatoes and salad.

▊ COOK'S TIP

*To use lower-calorie ox or
pig liver, cut it in slices and
soak overnight in skimmed
milk with a teaspoonful of
bicarbonate of soda; it will
be much improved.*

▊ COOK'S TIP

*If you know your guests
like liver, this way of
cooking the finest – and
most expensive – variety is
perfect for a dinner party. It
has to be cooked just before*
*serving but you can prepare
everything in advance.*

139 LIVER IN ORANGE SAUCE

Preparation time:
10 minutes

Cooking time:
8-10 minutes

Serves 4

Calories:
295 per portion

YOU WILL NEED:
4 *thin slices lamb's liver, about*
   100 g/4 oz each
2 *tablespoons seasoned flour for*
   coating
15 *g/½ oz butter*
1 *tablespoon olive oil*
4 *shallots, finely chopped*
150 *ml/¼ pint orange juice*
1 *teaspoon finely grated orange rind*
salt and pepper
2 *tablespoons chopped parsley*
FOR THE GARNISH
orange slices
parsley sprigs

Toss the liver in the seasoned flour, shaking off any excess. Heat the butter and oil in a large non-stick frying pan and fry two pieces of liver at a time for 2 minutes on each side, until browned on the outside and pale pink inside. Transfer to a warmed serving dish and keep warm.

Add the shallots to the pan and cook for 2 minutes, without browning. Lower the heat, add the orange juice and rind and boil for 2 minutes, stirring. Season with salt and pepper to taste and stir in the parsley. Spoon over the liver, garnish with orange slices and parsley and serve immediately.

140 SAUTEED KIDNEYS WITH VEGETABLE JULIENNE

Preparation time:
20 minutes

Cooking time:
20 minutes

Serves 6

Calories:
167 per portion

YOU WILL NEED:
12 *lambs' kidneys, skinned, halved*
   and cored
2 *teaspoons seasoned flour*
1 *small onion, chopped*
1 *tablespoon olive oil*
3 *carrots, peeled and cut into julienne*
   strips
2 *leeks, cleaned and cut into julienne*
   strips
100 *g/4 oz button mushrooms, thinly*
   sliced
150 *ml/¼ pint beef stock*
4 *tablespoons dry sherry*
salt and pepper
FOR THE GARNISH
julienne strips of carrot, blanched
julienne strips of leek, blanched

Dust the lambs' kidneys very lightly with seasoned flour. Fry the onion gently in the oil for 3-4 minutes, add the kidneys and fry until sealed on all sides.

Add the strips of carrot and leek and the sliced mushrooms and fry together for 1 minute. Stir in the stock and sherry and bring to the boil; add salt and pepper to taste, and simmer gently until the kidneys are just tender (12-15 minutes).

Serve garnished with the blanched strips of carrot and leek.

▥ COOK'S TIP

Put the seasoned flour in a polythene bag, making sure it has no holes, add the slices of liver one at a time and toss until coated lightly. This way the flour will not *be blown all over the kitchen.*

▥ COOK'S TIP

If you buy kidneys from a butcher they may still be covered with suet. Cut this away and remove the skin easily by nicking with the tip of a pointed knife.

POULTRY & GAME

Provided that the fatty skin is removed, chicken is an ideal choice for a main course, being high in protein. Many of the recipes in this chapter feature chicken portions which are so easy to cook and can taste so good with fresh herbs, spices and citrus fruit. A few special recipes for game have also been included.

141 CHICKEN AND LEEKS

Preparation time:
20 minutes, plus standing

Cooking time:
5-6 minutes

Serves 4

Calories:
189 per portion

YOU WILL NEED:
½ cucumber
salt
350 g/12 oz boneless chicken breasts, skinned
2 tablespoons oil
3 leeks, thinly sliced diagonally
4 garlic cloves, thinly sliced
1 tablespoon light soy sauce
1 tablespoon dry sherry
1 dried red chilli, crumbled
1 tablespoon chopped coriander
coriander leaves, to garnish

Peel the cucumber, cut in half and remove the seeds with a teaspoon. Cut the flesh into 2.5 cm/1 inch cubes, put in a colander and sprinkle with salt. Set aside for 20 minutes, rinse well and drain.

Cut the chicken into 2.5 cm/1 inch cubes. Heat the oil in a non-stick frying pan, add the leeks and garlic and cook briskly for 30 seconds. Add the chicken cubes and marinade and cook for 3 minutes. Add the soy sauce, sherry and chilli and cook for a further 30 seconds. Stir in the cucumber and cook for 30 seconds.

Transfer to a warmed serving dish, sprinkle with the chopped coriander, garnish with coriander leaves and serve immediately.

142 POUSSINS WITH PEAS

Preparation time:
30 minutes

Cooking time:
55 minutes

Serves 6

Calories:
292 per portion

YOU WILL NEED:
1 tablespoon olive oil
18 very small onions, shallots, or large spring onions
3 garlic cloves, very finely chopped
3 fresh poussins, about 350 g/ 12 oz each, halved down the backbone
175 ml/6 fl oz dry white wine
350 ml/12 fl oz hot water
salt and pepper
1 kg/2 ¼ lb peas, shelled weight

Heat the oil in a large heavy-based non-stick frying pan and fry the garlic and onions until light golden, then remove.

Fry the poussins, turning frequently until sealed and browned all over, then add the wine. As soon as it boils, add the water and salt and pepper to taste. Cover and simmer for 20 minutes, then uncover and simmer for another 20 minutes, adding the peas and onions about 8 minutes before cooking is completed.

■ COOK'S TIP

Try eating Chinese dishes with chopsticks. Hold one stick firmly in the angle between your thumb and first finger, balancing it against the first joint of your third finger. The second stick is held between the top of your thumb and the inside of your forefinger and is pivoted to pick up pieces of food.

■ COOK'S TIP

Frozen peas are much higher in fibre than fresh ones. Fibre is considered to be a good means of maintaining good health. It is only found in foods of vegetable origin.

143 BRAISED SPRING CHICKEN

Preparation time:
10 minutes

Cooking time:
1 hour 5 minutes

Oven temperature:
200°C, 400°F, gas 6

Serves 4

Calories:
626 per portion

YOU WILL NEED:
4 large flat mushrooms
2 teaspoons chopped fresh thyme
4 slices lean ham, without fat
2 spring chickens, prepared
salt and pepper
150 ml/¼ pint dry white wine

Cut off the mushroom stalks and place the mushrooms in the bottom of a large casserole. Sprinkle over the thyme. Lay the slices of ham over the mushrooms. Place the spring chickens on top. Add salt, pepper and the white wine.

Cover and cook in the oven for about 1 hour. Uncover and continue cooking for 5 minutes.

Cut each spring chicken in half and serve on a bed of mushrooms and ham.

144 SURPRISE SPRING CHICKEN

Preparation time:
15 minutes, plus marinating

Cooking time:
1½ hours

Oven temperature:
190°C, 375°F, gas 5

Serves 4

Calories:
351 per portion

YOU WILL NEED:
2 limes
1 small onion, cut into 8 slices
1 x 1-1.25 kg/2¼-2¾ lb spring
  chicken, prepared
25 g/1 oz raisins
2 tablespoons olive oil
pinch of chilli powder
sea salt
FOR THE GARNISH
lime slices
onion slices

Slash one lime almost through in 8 places and insert an onion slice in each cut. Place inside the chicken cavity with the raisins.

Squeeze the juice from the remaining lime and mix with the oil, chilli powder and salt to taste. Pour over the chicken and leave to marinate for 1 hour.

Truss the chicken securely and place in a roasting pan. Cook in the oven for 1½ hours, basting twice, or until the juices run clear yellow.

Serve the chicken with its juices on a bed of noodles. Garnish with lime and onion slices.

■ COOK'S TIP

If fresh thyme is not available, replace with half the quantity of dried thyme. This herb retains its aroma for quite a long time after drying but fresh thyme does, of course, have a better flavour.

■ COOK'S TIP

Always remove the giblets from a fresh chicken as soon as possible. Use the giblets immediately to make stock which can be frozen, if liked.

145 CHICKEN WITH SESAME SEEDS

Preparation time:
15 minutes, plus
standing

Cooking time:
5 minutes

Serves 4

Calories:
208 per portion

YOU WILL NEED:
350 g/12 oz boneless chicken breasts
1 egg white
½ teaspoon salt
2 teaspoons cornflour
2 tablespoons white sesame seeds
2 tablespoons oil
1 tablespoon dark soy sauce
1 tablespoon wine vinegar
½ teaspoon chilli bean sauce
½ teaspoon sesame oil
½ teaspoon roasted Szechuan
  peppercorns
4 spring onions, chopped

Cut the chicken into 7.5 cm/3 inch long shreds. Combine the egg white, salt and cornflour, toss in the chicken and mix thoroughly. Leave to stand for 15 minutes.

Cook the sesame seeds in a large non-stick frying pan until they are golden brown. Remove from the pan and set aside.

Heat the oil in the pan, add the chicken and stir-fry briskly for 1 minute. Remove with a slotted spoon. Add the soy sauce, vinegar, chilli bean sauce, sesame oil and peppercorns to the pan and bring to the boil. Add the chicken and spring onions and cook for 2 minutes. Sprinkle with the sesame seeds and serve immediately.

146 CITRUS CHICKEN

Preparation time:
10 minutes

Cooking time:
1 hour

Oven temperature:
190°C, 375°F, gas 5

Serves 4

Calories:
346 per portion

YOU WILL NEED:
4 chicken quarters, about 225 g/ 8 oz
  each, skinned
salt and pepper
ground cinnamon
2 large lemons or limes
2 large oranges
15 g/½ oz butter
parsley sprigs, to garnish

Rub the chicken quarters with salt and pepper and a little cinnamon. Place in a lightly oiled casserole.

Squeeze the juice from one of the lemons or limes and pour over the chicken. Grate the rind from one of the oranges. Peel the remaining lemon or lime and both oranges and chop the flesh. Mix the flesh with the grated orange rind and pour over the chicken. Dot the chicken and fruit with the butter.

Cover tightly and cook in the oven for 1 hour, or until tender. Garnish with parsley.

■ COOK'S TIP

There are considerable regional variations in Chinese cooking depending on the climate and what crops are grown. Szechuan province, on the Tibetan border, is renowned for its fiery dishes such as this one.

■ COOK'S TIP

Limes are slightly sweeter and have a more subtle flavour than lemons. You can tell a fresh lime by its dark, glossy, tight skin.

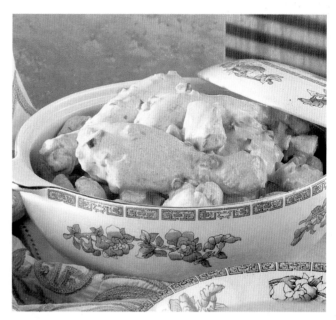

147 WEST INDIAN CHICKEN

Preparation time:
20 minutes, plus
marinating

Cooking time:
25 minutes

Serves 4

Calories:
215 per portion

YOU WILL NEED:
4 chicken portions, about 175 g/ 6 oz
   each, skinned
1 teaspoon curry powder, or to taste
1 teaspoon ground ginger
1 x 225 g/8 oz can pineapple chunks
   in natural juice
1 green pepper, seeded and chopped
salt and pepper

Score the flesh of the chicken portions with a sharp knife. Mix
the curry powder and ginger together and rub into the chicken
flesh. Place the chicken portions in a shallow dish and pour
over the pineapple juice from the can. Leave to marinate for 2
hours.

Put the chicken portions under a hot grill and cook for
about 20 minutes until tender, turning frequently and using
the marinade to baste and prevent burning.

Put the pineapple chunks, remaining marinade and
chopped pepper into a blender and liquidize until smooth.
Pour the purée into a pan and heat through. Taste and adjust
the seasoning.

Arrange the grilled chicken portions on a warmed serving
dish and pour the sauce over or serve it separately. Serve with
a green salad.

■ COOK'S TIP

Although the pineapple is
native to the Guyanas and
Brazil, it has been grown in
Jamaica for many years.
Fresh fruit is used there to
make this chicken dish but

the canned variety involves
less preparation.

148 SPICED CHICKEN

Preparation time:
15 minutes, plus
marinating

Cooking time:
1¼ hours

Serves 6

Calories:
240 per portion

YOU WILL NEED:
1 teaspoon ground cinnamon
6 chicken drumsticks, skinned
3 chicken breasts, about 175 g/ 6 oz
   each, boned and skinned
300 ml/½ pint natural low-fat yogurt
1 tablespoon oil
2 large onions, chopped
2 fresh green chillies, seeded and
   chopped
1 teaspoon cumin seeds
1 garlic clove, chopped
1 tablespoon sweet paprika
2 tablespoons chicken stock
½ teaspoon finely grated lemon rind
1 red pepper, seeded and chopped
1 tablespoon cornflour
salt and pepper

Rub the cinnamon into the chicken meat, combine with the
yogurt and marinate for about 30 minutes.

Heat the oil in a flameproof casserole and lightly fry the
onions, chillies, cumin and garlic. Stir in the paprika.

Strain the chicken meat, reserving the yogurt. Add the
chicken to the casserole, stir well to coat and then add the
stock, lemon rind, red pepper and half of the reserved yogurt.
Cover and simmer slowly for about 1 hour.

A few minutes before serving, combine the cornflour with
the remaining yogurt and stir it into the casserole, bring to the
boil and simmer for 1-2 minutes. Taste and add salt and pepper. Serve with rice.

■ COOK'S TIP

If you like spicy foods, try
keeping a dried chilli in the
storage jar with the rice. It
will impart its distinctive
flavour in the same way as a
vanilla pod kept in sugar.

149 CHICKEN WITH HERBS AND RICE

Preparation time:
20 minutes

Cooking time:
1¼ hours

Serves 4

Calories:
395 per portion

YOU WILL NEED:
2 tablespoons oil
1 onion, chopped
2 garlic cloves, chopped
4 chicken portions
100 g/4 oz mushrooms, sliced
150 ml/¼ pint chicken stock
150 ml/¼ pint dry cider
2 teaspoons chopped fresh mixed
  herbs
salt and pepper
100 g/4 oz long-grain rice
pinch of powdered saffron

Heat the oil in a non-stick frying pan. Fry the onion and garlic with the chicken portions until golden. Add the mushrooms, stock, cider, herbs and salt and pepper. Cover and simmer gently for 1 hour.

Meanwhile cook the rice (see Cook's Tip). Stir the saffron into the cooked rice.

To serve, arrange the rice on a warmed serving dish, put the chicken pieces and vegetables on top.

150 CASHEW CHICKEN

Preparation time:
20 minutes

Cooking time:
3-4 minutes

Serves 4

Calories:
208 per portion

YOU WILL NEED:
350 g/12 oz boneless chicken breasts,
  skinned
1 egg white
2 tablespoons dry sherry
2 teaspoons cornflour
2 tablespoons oil
4 spring onions, chopped
2 garlic cloves, thinly sliced
1 x 2.5 cm/1 inch piece root ginger,
  finely chopped
1 tablespoon light soy sauce
50 g/2 oz unsalted cashew nuts

Cut the chicken into 1 cm/½ inch cubes. Combine the egg white, half the sherry and the cornflour, add the chicken and toss well until evenly coated.

Heat the oil in a wok or large non-stick frying pan, add the spring onions, garlic and ginger and stir fry for 30 seconds. Add the chicken and cook for 2 minutes. Pour in the remaining sherry and the soy sauce and stir well. Add the cashew nuts and cook for a further 30 seconds. Serve immediately.

▥ COOK'S TIP

To cook the rice, put it in a saucepan with 300 ml/½ pint cold water. Bring to the boil, then cover and simmer for 15-20 minutes, until the water has been absorbed and the rice is tender. Do not lift the lid while the rice is cooking.

▥ COOK'S TIP

There are two basic designs of wok: one with a short, round handle on either side and one with a long handle. The former is better for steaming.

151 CHICKEN AND VEGETABLE CASSEROLE

Preparation time:
25 minutes

Cooking time:
1½ hours

Oven temperature:
180°C, 350°F, gas 4

Serves 4

Calories:
265 per portion

YOU WILL NEED:
1 onion, roughly chopped
3-4 celery sticks, roughly chopped
4 carrots, peeled and roughly chopped
4 turnips, peeled and roughly chopped
1 small swede, peeled and roughly
  chopped
4 chicken portions, about 175 g/ 6 oz
  each, skinned
1 bay leaf
1 bouquet garni (see Recipe 109)
300 ml/½ pint chicken stock
salt and pepper

Put half of the vegetables in a casserole. Put the chicken portions on top and cover with the remaining vegetables. Add the bay leaf, bouquet garni, stock, salt and pepper to taste. If using a flameproof casserole, bring to the boil on top of the cooker and skim.

Cover and cook in the oven for about 1½ hours. Skim off any fat and serve.

152 CHICKEN IN LEMON SAUCE

Preparation time:
20 minutes

Cooking time:
1 hour 10 minutes

Oven temperature:
190°C, 375°F, gas 5

Serves 4

Calories:
228 per portion

YOU WILL NEED:
4 chicken portions, about 175 g/ 6 oz
  each, skinned
grated rind and juice of 1 lemon
1 small onion, chopped
1 celery stick, chopped
few thyme sprigs
salt and pepper
300 ml/½ pint chicken stock
15 g/½ oz cornflour
FOR THE GARNISH
watercress
lemon twists

Put the chicken in a 1.75 litre/3 pint casserole. Add the lemon rind and juice, onion, celery, thyme, salt and pepper to taste, and the stock. Cover and cook in the oven for 1 hour, or until the chicken is tender.

Transfer the chicken to a serving dish and keep hot. Strain the stock.

Mix the cornflour to a smooth paste with a little of the stock. Then combine with the remaining stock and cook over a low heat, stirring constantly, until thickened. Check the seasoning and pour the sauce over the chicken. Garnish with watercress and lemon.

▨ COOK'S TIP

If you cook this casserole the day before, it can be put in the refrigerator overnight and reheated for 30 minutes before serving. The fat is easier to remove when cold.

▨ COOK'S TIP

Using cornflour to thicken sauces rather than butter and flour cuts calories. Thicken clear sauces with potato flour as this will not cloud the sauce.

153 CHICKEN IN SWEET AND SOUR SAUCE

Preparation time:
20 minutes

Cooking time:
1 hour

Oven temperature:
190°C, 375°F, gas 5

Serves 4

Calories:
264 per portion

YOU WILL NEED:
*4 chicken portions, about 175 g/ 6 oz
    each, skinned*
1 green pepper, seeded and chopped
1 red pepper, seeded and chopped
1 onion, sliced
*1 x 225 g/8 oz can pineapple pieces in
    natural juice, drained*
1 tablespoon soy sauce
1 tablespoon vinegar
1 x 225 g/8 oz can tomatoes
150 ml/¼ pint water
1 teaspoon clear honey
salt

Put the chicken portions in a 1.75 litre/3 pint casserole and cook, uncovered, in the oven for 15 minutes.

Put the remaining ingredients, with salt to taste, in a saucepan. Bring to the boil, stirring, cover and simmer for 20 minutes. Pour the sauce over the chicken and return to the oven for a further 30 minutes, or until the chicken is tender, basting occasionally with the sauce. Serve with green vegetables.

154 LEMON CHICKEN

Preparation time:
25 minutes

Cooking time:
30-35 minutes

Serves 4

Calories:
220 per portion

YOU WILL NEED:
*1 lemon, very thinly peeled, rind
    reserved*
1 small onion, thinly sliced
1 tablespoon olive oil
*4 chicken breasts, about 150 g/
    5 oz each, skinned and boned*
2 tablespoons chopped parsley
300 ml/½ pint chicken stock
salt and pepper
2 teaspoons cornflour
1 tablespoon water

Cut the lemon rind into matchstick strips. Halve the lemon and squeeze out the juice.

Fry the onion gently in the oil for 3-4 minutes, then add the chicken breasts and fry until lightly browned on all sides. Add the parsley, stock, salt and pepper to taste and lemon juice; cover the pan and simmer gently for 20 minutes. Remove the chicken breasts to a warmed serving dish, and keep hot.

Blend the cornflour and water to a smooth paste; stir in the hot cooking liquid, and then return to the pan. Stir over a gentle heat until thickened. Add the strips of lemon rind to the sauce and spoon evenly over the chicken.

■ COOK'S TIP

The natural sweetness of pineapple makes it a perfect fruit to use in sweet'n'sour dishes. It combines particularly well with chicken and the other ingredients in this appetizing casserole.

■ COOK'S TIP

Lemons can be stored for some weeks in the crisper drawer of a refrigerator, so buy in quantity during their peak season. The smooth-skinned variety are juicier.

155 CARIBBEAN CHICKEN

Preparation time: 15 minutes	YOU WILL NEED: 4 chicken portions, about 175 g/ 6 oz each, skinned
Cooking time: 1 hour	1 large red pepper, seeded and chopped
Oven temperature: 220°C, 425°F, gas 7	1 teaspoon curry powder 250 ml/8 fl oz chicken stock salt and pepper
Serves 4	4 pineapple rings, fresh or canned in natural juice
Calories: 284 per portion	1 banana 1 orange, peeled and sliced, to garnish

Put the chicken portions in a casserole with the chopped pepper and curry powder. Pour over the stock and add salt and pepper to taste. Cover and cook in the oven for 50 minutes.

Chop the pineapple rings and banana and add to the casserole. Cook for a further 10 minutes, or until the chicken is tender.

Garnish the casserole with the orange slices.

156 SPICY CHICKEN AND PEANUTS

Preparation time: 20 minutes	YOU WILL NEED: 50 g/2 oz unsalted peanuts
Cooking time: 5 minutes	350 g/12 oz boneless chicken breasts, skinned 2 tablespoons oil
Serves 4	1 dried red chilli 1 tablespoon dry sherry
Calories: 272 per portion	1 tablespoon dark soy sauce pinch of sugar 1 garlic clove, crushed 2 spring onions, chopped 1 x 2.5 cm/1 inch piece root ginger, finely chopped 1 teaspoon wine vinegar 2 teaspoons sesame oil red chilli flowers (see Cook's Tip)

Immerse the peanuts in a bowl of boiling water for about 2 minutes. Drain well, remove the skins and put on absorbent kitchen paper to dry thoroughly. Cut the chicken into 2.5 cm/1 inch cubes.

Heat the oil in a large non-stick frying pan. Crumble in the chilli, add the chicken and peanuts and stir-fry for 1 minute; remove from the pan. Add the sherry, soy sauce, sugar, garlic, spring onions, ginger and vinegar to the pan. Bring to the boil, then simmer for 30 seconds. Return the chicken, chilli and peanuts to the pan and cook for 2 minutes. Sprinkle over the sesame oil. Pile into a warmed serving dish, garnish with red chilli flowers and serve immediately.

▓ COOK'S TIP

Curry powder can be made at home with freshly ground spices such as coriander seeds, turmeric, fenugreek, ginger, black pepper, cardamom and cinnamon.

▓ COOK'S TIP

To make chilli flowers, shred the chilli lengthways leaving 1 cm/½ inch attached at the stem end. Put in a bowl of iced water for about 1 hour to open.

157 SLIMMER'S COQ AU VIN

Preparation time:
20 minutes, plus
marinating

Cooking time:
1 hour 10 minutes

Oven temperature:
220°C, 425°F, gas 7

Serves 4

Calories:
274 per portion

YOU WILL NEED:
4 chicken portions, about 175 g/ 6 oz
*   each, skinned*
2 tablespoons brandy
225 g/8 oz baby onions, peeled
900 ml/1½ pints chicken stock
225 g/8 oz button mushrooms, wiped
*   and trimmed*
chopped fresh parsley, to garnish
FOR THE MARINADE
1 garlic clove, crushed
150 ml/¼ pint red wine vinegar
150 ml/¼ pint red wine
1 tablespoon Worcestershire sauce
salt and pepper

Combine all the marinade ingredients. Put the chicken in a
large shallow bowl and pour over the marinade. Set aside in a
cool place for at least 3 hours.

Remove the chicken portions from the marinade (reserving
the marinade), and brown briefly under the grill. Transfer the
chicken to a casserole. Pour the brandy over the chicken and
ignite. When the flames die, add the onions and stock. Cover
and cook in the oven for 50 minutes. Add the mushrooms and
cook for 10 minutes, or until the chicken is tender and the
juices run clear.

Meanwhile, pour the marinade into a saucepan and boil
rapidly, uncovered, until reduced in volume by half. Stir into
the casserole and garnish with the parsley.

158 ITALIAN CHICKEN

Preparation time:
25 minutes

Cooking time:
1 hour

Oven temperature:
180°C, 350°F, gas 4

Serves 4

Calories:
274 per portion

YOU WILL NEED:
4 chicken breasts, skinned and boned
50 g/2 oz lean ham, cut into 4 pieces
150 ml/¼ pint chicken stock
1 red pepper, seeded and sliced
watercress sprigs, to garnish
FOR THE STUFFING
40 g/1½ oz wholemeal breadcrumbs
25 g/1 oz Parmesan cheese, grated
1 small onion, finely chopped
2 teaspoons chopped parsley
1 tablespoon dry sherry
salt and pepper

Mix together the stuffing ingredients, with salt and pepper to
taste, and press to the underside of the chicken breasts. Place
a piece of ham over the top. Arrange the chicken in a casserole, pour over the stock and add the red pepper.

Cover and cook in the oven for 1 hour, or until the chicken
is cooked, basting occasionally with the liquid. Garnish with
watercress.

■ COOK'S TIP

*Mushrooms are best stored
in the refrigerator in a
paper or fabric bag. If you
have bought them loose,
avoid leaving them in a
plastic bag.*

■ COOK'S TIP

*Freshly grated Parmesan
would always be used by
any Italian who prided
themselves on their cooking.
Most large supermarkets
now sell small blocks of*
*Parmesan as well as drums
of the grated kind.*

159 POULET CHASSEUR

Preparation time:
25 minutes

Cooking time:
1½ hours

Serves 6

Calories:
416 per portion

YOU WILL NEED:
2 tablespoons oil
1 x 1.75 kg/4 lb chicken, cut into
    serving pieces
100 g/4 oz baby onions
250 g/8 oz shallots, chopped
150 ml/¼ pint dry vermouth
1 bouquet garni (see Recipe 109)
1 bay leaf
salt and pepper
1 x 400 g/14 oz can tomatoes
225 g/8 oz button mushrooms
1 tablespoon tomato purée

Heat the oil in a non-stick frying pan, add the chicken pieces and fry until browned on all sides. Remove from the pan. Add the onions and shallots to the pan and cook for 5 minutes.

Remove the pan from the heat, add the vermouth and ignite. When the flames have died down, return the chicken to the pan and add the bouquet garni, bay leaf, and salt and pepper to taste. Add the tomatoes with their juice, bring to the boil, cover and simmer for 1 hour.

Add the mushrooms and tomato purée and cook, uncovered, for 20-30 minutes, until the sauce is reduced and thickened. Serve immediately.

▨ COOK'S TIP

*For authenticity, use a
French vermouth. This is
drier than the Italian. If you
warm the vermouth before
igniting it, it will be more
effective.*

160 PIMENTO CHICKEN

Preparation time:
1 hour

Cooking time:
2¼ hours

Serves 8

Calories:
315 per portion

YOU WILL NEED:
1 x 1.75 kg/4 lb oven-ready chicken
1 onion, quartered
1 carrot, sliced
2 celery sticks, sliced
4 juniper berries, crushed
1 bay leaf
4-6 stalks parsley
salt
6 peppercorns, lightly crushed
FOR THE SAUCE
225 g/8 oz canned pimentos, drained,
    rinsed and chopped
1 tablespoon tomato purée
2 tablespoons mango chutney
200 ml/7 fl oz low-fat yogurt
freshly ground black pepper

Put the chicken, vegetables, juniper berries, bay leaf, parsley, salt and peppercorns into a saucepan. Cover with water. Bring to the boil, cover the saucepan and simmer for 1½-2 hours, or until the chicken is tender. Leave the chicken to cool in the stock. Lift out the chicken, drain and dry it. (Reserve the stock, discarding the bay leaf.) Skin the chicken and slice the meat from the bones.

To make the sauce, put the pimentos, 2 tablespoons of the reserved chicken stock, tomato purée and chutney into a saucepan and bring to the boil. Liquidize in a blender and set aside to cool. Blend the cooled pimento mixture with the yogurt and season with salt and pepper.

Arrange the chicken on a dish and cover with the sauce.

▨ COOK'S TIP

*This is an excellent way of
serving chicken at a summer
lunch party as it can be
prepared in advance. Serve
with a choice of colourful
salads to complement it.*

161 CHICKEN WITH YOGURT

Preparation time:
20 minutes

Cooking time:
1 hour 10 minutes

Serves 4

Calories:
491 per portion

YOU WILL NEED:
1 x 1.5 kg/3 lb chicken
1 onion, chopped
1 garlic clove, crushed
½ green pepper, seeded and chopped
2 tablespoons oil
25 g/1 oz cornflour
600 ml/1 pint chicken stock
salt and pepper
300 ml/½ pint natural low-fat yogurt
FOR THE GARNISH
chopped fresh chives or parsley

Cut the chicken into portions. Heat the oil in a flameproof casserole or saucepan. Add the chicken pieces, onion, green pepper and garlic and fry the chicken until lightly browned on all sides.

Mix the cornflour to a smooth paste with a little of the stock. Then combine with the remaining stock and cook over a low heat, stirring constantly until thickened. Pour over the chicken, cover the casserole or saucepan and simmer for 30 minutes. Stir in the yogurt and continue cooking gently for 30 minutes. Adjust the seasoning to taste before serving. Sprinkle lightly with chopped chives or parsley.

162 CHICKEN WITH GINGER

Preparation time:
20 minutes, plus marinating

Cooking time:
4-5 minutes

Serves 4

Calories:
182 per portion

YOU WILL NEED:
350 g/12 oz boneless chicken breasts, skinned
1 tablespoon dry sherry
4 spring onions, chopped
1 x 2.5 cm/1 inch piece fresh root ginger, finely chopped
2 tablespoons oil
1-2 garlic cloves, thinly sliced
2 celery sticks, sliced diagonally
1 small green pepper, seeded and sliced
2 tablespoons light soy sauce
juice of ½ lemon
shredded rind of 2 lemons
¼ teaspoon chilli powder
FOR THE GARNISH
lemon slices
parsley sprigs

Cut the chicken into 7.5 cm/3 inch strips. Combine the sherry, spring onions and ginger, add the chicken and toss well to coat, then set aside for 15 minutes.

Heat the oil in a large non-stick frying pan or wok. Add the garlic, celery and green pepper and stir-fry for 1 minute. Add the chicken and marinade and cook for 2 minutes. Stir in the soy sauce, lemon juice and rind and chilli powder and cook for a further 1 minute.

Pile into a warmed serving dish, garnish with lemon slices and parsley sprigs and serve immediately.

■ COOK'S TIP

A garlic press is the easiest way of crushing the cloves. Remove stubborn threads of garlic from the holes in the press with a pin.

■ COOK'S TIP

If you cannot find any fresh root ginger locally, use the dried kind. The best quality ginger comes from Jamaica and is usually available in markets supplying ethnic communities, as well as in some large supermarkets.

163 TURKEY FILLETS WITH PIQUANT PRAWN SAUCE

Preparation time:
25 minutes

Cooking time:
30-35 minutes

Oven temperature:
190-200°C, 375-400°F, gas 5-6

Serves 6

Calories:
243 per portion

YOU WILL NEED:
3 red peppers, seeded and chopped
1 chilli, seeded and cut into 6
3 garlic cloves, chopped
3 tomatoes, peeled, seeded and
 chopped
1 aubergine, finely chopped
salt and pepper
6 turkey fillets, about 175 g/6 oz each
1 tablespoon olive oil
1 tablespoon vinegar
1 teaspoon anchovy essence
175 g/6 oz peeled, cooked prawns

Put all the chopped vegetables in a bowl, sprinkle with salt and pepper, and mix well. Spread the mixture over a sheet of foil large enough to lay the turkey fillets on side by side. Put the fillets on top of the vegetables and paint with a little of the oil. Cover loosely with more foil and seal completely. Cook on a baking sheet in the preheated oven (the oven temperature depending on the thickness of the fillets), for 25-30 minutes. Remove the fillets to a warmed serving dish.

Heat the remaining oil in a saucepan and rub the cooked vegetables through a sieve on to it. Bring to the boil and add the vinegar, anchovy essence and prawns, adjust the seasoning and cook for 3-5 minutes. Spoon the sauce over the fillets.

164 GINGERED TURKEY

Preparation time:
10 minutes, plus
soaking

Cooking time:
10 minutes

Serves 4

Calories:
225 per portion

YOU WILL NEED:
225 g/8 oz dried apricots
1-2 teaspoons ground ginger
4 turkey fillets, about 100 g/4 oz each

Put the apricots in a bowl. Just cover with water and add the ground ginger. Leave to soak overnight.

Next day, put the turkey fillets on the rack of a grill pan and spoon over a little of the apricot soaking liquid. Put under a hot grill for about 10 minutes, turning once. If necessary, spoon over more apricot liquid.

Meanwhile, simmer the apricots in the rest of the soaking liquid for about 10 minutes. Pour the cooked apricots into a blender and liquidize until smooth.

Arrange the cooked turkey fillets on a warmed serving dish and pour the apricot sauce over. Serve with green beans.

■ COOK'S TIP

Penne – the pasta that is shaped like a quill – or plain rice, mixed with a little diced cucumber, make good accompaniments to these turkey fillets.

■ COOK'S TIP

Dried apricots are one of the best sources of fibre. None of this is lost by liquidizing the fruit. They give a delicious flavour to the turkey fillets.

165 SWEET-SOUR CHINESE TURKEY

Preparation time:
15 minutes, plus marinating

Cooking time:
15-20 minutes

Serves 4

Calories:
180 per portion

YOU WILL NEED:
450 g/1 lb turkey breast
2 tablespoons lemon juice
5 tablespoons orange juice
4-5 celery sticks
2 sharon fruit or firm tomatoes
8-10 radishes
½ Chinese cabbage
1 large green pepper, seeded
2 tablespoons oil
150 ml/¼ pint chicken stock
1½ teaspoons cornflour
1 tablespoon soy sauce
1 tablespoon clear honey

Cut the turkey breast into thin strips. Marinate in the lemon and orange juice for 30 minutes. Cut the celery, sharon fruit or tomatoes, radishes and Chinese cabbage into small neat pieces. Heat the oil in a large non-stick frying pan. Drain the turkey and reserve the marinade. Fry the turkey in the oil until nearly tender. Add the vegetables and sharon fruit or tomatoes and heat for 2-3 minutes only. Blend the chicken stock with the marinade and the cornflour. Add the soy sauce and sugar. Pour over the ingredients in the pan and stir until thickened.

166 TURKEY-STUFFED AUBERGINES

Preparation time:
15 minutes, plus draining

Cooking time:
35 minutes

Oven temperature:
200°C, 400°F, gas 6

Serves 4

Calories:
194 per portion

YOU WILL NEED:
2 large aubergines
lemon juice
salt and pepper
100 g/4 oz macaroni, cooked
350 g/12 oz cooked turkey meat, cut
*   into chunks*
300 ml/½ pint tomato juice
1 teaspoon ground coriander
parsley sprigs, to garnish

Cut each aubergine in half and sprinkle with lemon juice and salt. Leave to drain for at least 30 minutes.

Put each half on a piece of foil large enough to enclose it completely. Wrap the aubergine halves and cook in the oven for about 30 minutes.

Meanwhile, gently heat the macaroni and turkey meat in the tomato juice, coriander and salt and pepper to taste.

When the aubergines are tender, unwrap and carefully scoop out the flesh. Mix with the macaroni and turkey pieces and pile back into the aubergine shells. Return to the oven to heat through for 5 minutes. Serve immediately, sprinkled with parsley.

■ COOK'S TIP

Sharon fruit is a variety of persimmon which can be eaten like an apple. The skin is edible or the fruit can be peeled. It is often candied.

■ COOK'S TIP

This is an appetizing way of using turkey leftovers. Turkey portions are easily available and some delicatessens and food shops also sell cooked turkey *pieces. Remember to remove all the skin.*

167 SESAME TURKEY WITH GINGER AND LYCHEES

Preparation time:
25 minutes

Cooking time:
15-20 minutes

Serves 4

Calories:
288 per portion

YOU WILL NEED:
450 g/1 lb turkey fillets, cut into thin
    strips
1 egg, beaten
3 tablespoons sesame seeds
3 tablespoons olive oil
1 small onion, finely chopped
1 garlic clove, finely chopped
slice of fresh root ginger, 1 cm/ 1/2 inch
    thick, peeled and chopped
2 tablespoons unsweetened pineapple
    juice
4 tablespoons chicken stock
12 fresh lychees, shelled
1 tablespoon lime juice
salt and pepper
julienne strips of spring onion, to
    garnish

Dip the strips of turkey into beaten egg, shaking off the excess, and coat lightly in sesame seeds.

Heat the olive oil in a shallow pan; add the onion and garlic and fry for 2-3 minutes. Add the ginger and the strips of turkey and fry until the turkey is evenly coloured. Pour over the pineapple juice and stock and simmer for 5 minutes, covered. Add the lychees and lime juice and season well to taste. Stir well, then simmer, covered, for a further 4-5 minutes. Serve, garnished with spring onion strips, on a bed of Chinese noodles.

168 TURKEY WITH WALNUTS

Preparation time:
25 minutes

Cooking time:
8-10 minutes

Serves 4

Calories:
152 per portion

YOU WILL NEED:
1 tablespoon oil
1 onion, finely chopped
1 garlic clove, crushed
1 turkey breast, skinned, sliced and
    cut into small slivers
grated rind and juice of 1 orange
25 g/1 oz walnuts, chopped
1 tablespoon soy sauce
2 teaspoons cornflour, blended with 4
    tablespoons water
1 teaspoon clear honey
1 tablespoon finely chopped parsley
pepper
orange rind, shredded, to garnish

Heat the oil in a non-stick frying pan, add the onion and fry, stirring for 2 minutes. Stir in the garlic and push the mixture to one side of the pan. Tilt the pan to let the juices run out over the base. Add the turkey slivers and stir-fry for about 2 minutes. Remove with a slotted spoon and keep warm in a warmed serving dish.

Add the orange rind and juice, walnuts, soy sauce, blended cornflour, sugar and parsley to the pan. Bring to the boil, stirring, then simmer until thickened. Add pepper to taste and pour over the turkey. Garnish with orange rind.

■ COOK'S TIP

The stones can be removed
from the lychees before
adding to the casserole but
do this in a dish so that
none of the fragrant juice is
wasted.

■ COOK'S TIP

Walnuts do not keep well as
their oil tends to go rancid.
They should therefore be
bought in small quantities
and used as soon as
possible. When they are
really fresh, the skin
enclosing the kernel can
easily be removed.

169 TURKEY SICILIAN-STYLE

Preparation time:
20 minutes

Cooking time:
30 minutes

Serves 4

Calories:
209 per portion

YOU WILL NEED:
25 g/1 oz butter
1 onion, sliced
75 g/3 oz button mushrooms, sliced
25 g/1 oz plain wholemeal flour
½ teaspoon ground ginger
½ teaspoon grated nutmeg
150 ml/¼ pint chicken stock
150 ml/¼ pint skimmed milk
350 g/12 oz cooked turkey meat,
    chopped
salt and pepper
15 g/½ oz flaked almonds, toasted

Melt the butter in a large saucepan, add the onion and mushrooms and fry gently for 5 minutes, or until soft. Add the flour, ginger and nutmeg. Cook for 1 minute. Gradually blend in the stock and milk. Bring to the boil, stirring, then add the turkey and salt and pepper to taste. Cover and simmer for 20 minutes.

Pile the mixture into a warmed serving dish and sprinkle with the toasted almonds. Serve with a small portion of noodles and salad.

170 TURKEY PORTUGAISE

Preparation time:
15 minutes

Cooking time:
20 minutes

Oven temperature:
220°C, 425°F, gas 7

Serves 4

Calories:
131 per portion

YOU WILL NEED:
4 turkey fillets, about 100 g/4 oz each
1 garlic clove, crushed
2 tomatoes, roughly chopped
1 carrot, peeled and very thinly sliced
25 g/1 oz onion, chopped
salt and pepper

Put each turkey fillet on a piece of foil large enough to cover it. Spread a little crushed garlic on each one. Divide the tomato, carrot and onion between the fillets. Sprinkle with salt and pepper. Wrap the fillets completely in foil and cook in the oven for about 20 minutes until tender.

■ COOK'S TIP

With such a large variety of fresh pasta now available, it is easy to experiment with different kinds. Children will like the new novelty shapes like rockets.

■ COOK'S TIP

For family meals the turkey could be served in the packages. A green salad is a suitable accompaniment.

171 DICED TURKEY WITH CELERY

Preparation time:
25 minutes, plus soaking

Cooking time:
3 minutes

Serves 4

Calories:
224 per portion

YOU WILL NEED:
4 Chinese dried mushrooms
350 g/12 oz boneless turkey breast, skinned and diced
salt
1 egg white
1 tablespoon cornflour
2 tablespoons oil
2 garlic cloves, sliced
2 slices root ginger, chopped
2 leeks, diagonally sliced
1 small head celery, diagonally sliced
1 red pepper, seeded and sliced
3 tablespoons light soy sauce
2 tablespoons dry sherry

Soak the mushrooms in warm water for 15 minutes. Squeeze dry and discard the stalks, then slice the caps.

Season the diced turkey with salt, dip in the egg white, then coat with cornflour. Heat the oil in a large non-stick frying pan. Add the turkey and stir-fry for 1 minute, until golden brown. Remove with a slotted spoon and drain on absorbent kitchen paper.

Increase the heat, add the garlic, ginger, leeks and celery and stir-fry for 1 minute. Return the turkey to the pan, add the red pepper and stir-fry for 30 seconds. Stir in the soy sauce and sherry and cook for a further 30 seconds. Spoon into a warmed serving dish and serve immediately.

■ COOK'S TIP

Chinese dried mushrooms should be washed in lukewarm water before soaking.

172 TURKEY SALAD

Preparation time:
25 minutes

Serves 4

Calories:
330 per portion

YOU WILL NEED:
40 g/1½ oz hazelnuts
75 g/3 oz grapes, quartered and pipped
100 g/4 oz drained canned water chestnuts
225 g/8 oz Chinese leaves, finely shredded
450 g/1 lb cooked turkey meat, cut in bite-sized pieces
FOR THE DRESSING
2 teaspoons grated Parmesan cheese
1 egg
2 teaspoons olive, sunflower or walnut oil
2 teaspoons lemon or orange juice
pinch of mustard powder
1 garlic clove, crushed (optional)
pinch of black pepper
pinch of sea salt
few drops of Worcestershire sauce
150 ml/¼ pint natural low-fat yogurt

Put the hazelnuts in an ungreased heavy-based pan over a low heat for 2-3 minutes, stirring until lightly browned. Combine with all the other salad ingredients in a bowl.

Blend all the dressing ingredients except the yogurt in a liquidizer. Transfer to a jug. Mix the yogurt into the dressing with a wooden spoon and stir the dressing into the salad. Mix the salad ingredients well.

■ COOK'S TIP

Turkey is a very lean meat and can become rather dry after cooking. Avoid this happening by covering cooked turkey with stock before storing in the *refrigerator if preparing it in advance.*

173 TURKEY PORTIONS CREOLE

Preparation time:
20 minutes

Cooking time:
1½ hours

Serves 6

Calories:
209 per portion

YOU WILL NEED:
2 tablespoons plain flour
salt and pepper
750 g/1½ lb turkey portions
2 tablespoons oil
2 onions, sliced
1 green pepper, cored and seeded
1 garlic clove, crushed
1 x 400 g/14 oz can peeled chopped
    tomatoes
1 bouquet garni (see Recipe 109)
150 ml/¼ pint chicken stock
chopped parsley, to garnish

Season the flour and use to coat the turkey portions. Heat the oil lightly in a large flameproof casserole and fry the turkey portions until golden on all sides. Add the onion, garlic and green pepper to the turkey, lower the heat and cook gently for 5 minutes. Cook for a minute, then add the tomatoes and juice, bouquet garni and stock. Bring to the boil, stirring, cover tightly and simmer gently for 1¼ hours, or until the turkey portions are tender.

When cooked lift the turkey pieces on to a warmed serving dish and keep hot. Discard the bouquet garni and boil the sauce rapidly, uncovered, until reduced to a coating consistency. Adjust the seasoning to taste and pour over the turkey. Serve sprinkled with parsley.

▊ COOK'S TIP

This is a tasty and economical casserole for family meals. You can always add a little dry white wine to the stock if you want to serve it to guests.

174 TURKEY PARCELS

Preparation time:
35 minutes

Cooking time:
35 minutes

Serves 8

Calories:
224 per portion

YOU WILL NEED:
8 turkey escalopes, about 150 g/ 5 oz
    each
300 ml/½ pint white wine
300 ml/½ pint turkey or chicken stock
FOR THE STUFFING
225 g/8 oz courgettes, grated
50 g/2 oz hazelnuts, toasted and
    ground
2 spring onions, trimmed and finely
    chopped
½ tablespoon lime juice
1 teaspoon grated lime rind
1 teaspoon clear honey
1 teaspoon grated fresh ginger
1 teaspoon fresh or dried thyme
coarsely ground black pepper

Prepare the turkey escalopes (see Cook's Tip). Then combine all the stuffing ingredients together in a mixing bowl, adding black pepper to taste. Divide the stuffing between the escalopes, pushing it well into the pockets.

Combine the wine and stock. Pour into one or two large shallow pans and bring to the boil. Reduce to a very gentle simmer and poach the escalopes, stuffing side up, for 20-25 minutes, until cooked through. Remove the escalopes with a slotted spoon and drain on absorbent kitchen paper. Transfer to a warmed serving dish and keep warm.

Boil the poaching liquid fast until reduced to about 150 ml/¼ pint. Spoon a little of the reduced cooking juices over each escalope and serve.

▊ COOK'S TIP

With a sharp knife, cut a 5 cm/2 inch slit in each escalope pushing the knife deep into the flesh to make a pocket. Do not cut through the flesh.

175 TURKEY WITH BROCCOLI

Preparation time:
15 minutes

Cooking time:
20-25 minutes

Serves 4

Calories:
288 per portion

YOU WILL NEED:
*4 turkey breasts, about 100 g/4 oz
each*
450 g/1 lb broccoli
salt
FOR THE SAUCE
25 g/1 oz butter
1 garlic clove, peeled (optional)
2 teaspoons cornflour
300 ml/½ pint skimmed milk
300 ml/½ pint chicken stock
1 bay leaf
25 g/1 oz grated Parmesan cheese

Put the turkey breasts under a preheated hot grill and cook, turning, for about 15 minutes until tender.

Meanwhile, steam the broccoli for about 12 minutes until just tender. Arrange the broccoli on a warmed serving dish and place the turkey breasts on top. Keep hot.

To make the sauce, melt the butter in a saucepan and add the garlic. Cook gently for a few seconds then stir in the cornflour. Cook for 2 minutes, stirring. Remove the garlic. Add enough skimmed milk and chicken stock to make a thin sauce. Add the bay leaf and cook for a few minutes, stirring, until the sauce thickens. Remove the bay leaf. Pour over the turkey breasts and broccoli. Sprinkle with the Parmesan cheese and place under a preheated hot grill until lightly browned.

176 RABBIT CASSEROLE

Preparation time:
15 minutes

Cooking time:
1 hour 10 minutes

Oven temperature:
180°C, 350°F, gas 4

Serves 4

Calories:
329 per portion

YOU WILL NEED:
750 g/1 ½ lb rabbit joints
150 ml/¼ pint red wine
rind of 1 lemon
2 garlic cloves, crushed
bouquet garni (see Recipe 109)
100 g/4 oz lean cooked ham, cubed
225 g/8 oz onions, sliced
225 g/8 oz carrots, thinly sliced
150 g/5 oz button mushrooms, halved
1 tablespoon cornflour
¼ teaspoon cayenne
1 tablespoon redcurrant jelly

Put the rabbit, wine, water, lemon rind, garlic, herbs, ham, onion, carrot and salt in a flameproof casserole. Bring to simmering point, cover and cook in the oven for 35 minutes.

Add the mushrooms and cook for 15 minutes, or until the rabbit and vegetables are tender. Using a slotted spoon, transfer meat and vegetables to a warmed serving dish; keep hot.

Mix the cornflour to a smooth paste with a little of the liquid in the casserole. Add to the remaining liquid and cook, stirring over moderate heat, until thickened.

Add the cayenne and redcurrant jelly and cook for 3-4 minutes, until syrupy. Pour over the meat and vegetables.

■ COOK'S TIP

It is very easy to overcook broccoli so watch it carefully. Try leaving the lid balanced over the top of the steamer to allow some air to reach it.

■ COOK'S TIP

Traditionally, dumplings are served with this substantial casserole of the kind that farmers' wives used to make for their menfolk after a day's toil on the land. They *would probably have used cider instead of wine.*

177 FAISAN EN CASSEROLE

Preparation time:	YOU WILL NEED:
20 minutes	40 g/1 ½ oz butter
Cooking t̶	
2¾ hours	
	̶, ̶crushed
Oven temp̶.	450 ml/¾ pint beef stock
160°C, 325°F, gas 3	grated rind and juice of 1 orange
	150 ml/¼ pint red wine
Serves 6	1 bay leaf
	bouquet garni (see Recipe 109)
Calories:	salt and pepper
491 per portion	2 tablespoons cornflour

Melt the butter in a flameproof casserole, add the pheasant and fry until browned on all sides; remove from the casserole. Add the onions and garlic to the pan and cook gently for 10 minutes. Return the pheasant to the casserole, add the beef stock, orange rind and juice, herbs and salt and pepper to taste. Bring to the boil, then cook in the oven for 2½ hours, or until tender.

Transfer the pheasant to a warmed serving dish; keep hot. Mix the cornflour to a smooth paste with a little of the liquid in the casserole. Add to the remaining liquid and cook, stirring over moderate heat, until thickened. Spoon the sauce over the pheasant to serve.

178 PHEASANT WITH GREEN PEPPERCORNS

Preparation time:	YOU WILL NEED:
30 minutes, plus	2 medium pheasants
marinating	175 ml/6 fl oz unsweetened orange
	juice
Cooking time:	1 garlic clove, crushed
25-30 minutes	1 tablespoon chopped chives
	salt
Serves 8	2 teaspoons green peppercorns
Calories:	150 ml/¼ pint dry white wine
501 per portion	4 canned artichoke hearts
	FOR THE GARNISH
	heart-shaped croûtons
	peeled orange segments

Using a very sharp knife, remove the breasts and drumsticks from each bird. Put the pheasant in a dish with the orange juice, garlic, chives and salt. Cover and chill for 4 hours.

Transfer the pheasant and marinade to a large frying pan. Add the peppercorns and the white wine and simmer for 15-20 minutes. Add the artichoke hearts and simmer for a further 6-8 minutes, until the pheasant is just tender. Remove the pheasant and artichoke hearts and keep warm.

Reduce the cooking juices slightly over a brisk heat; spoon over the pheasant and garnish with the croûtons and orange segments.

■ COOK'S TIP

Unplucked game birds should be hung by the neck in a cool, airy place 3-10 days after they are shot, before being prepared for cooking or the freezer.

■ COOK'S TIP

Look for pheasants with bright, glossy plumage and smooth legs, which indicate young birds. The cocks should have short spurs.

179 WILD DUCK WITH SATSUMA SAUCE

Preparation time:	YOU WILL NEED:
20 minutes	5 satsumas
	1 small onion, finely chopped
Cooking time:	4 tablespoons unsweetened orange
1 hour 10 minutes	juice
	2 tablespoons dry vermouth
Oven temperature:	200 ml/7 fl oz chicken stock
190°C, 375°F, gas 5	salt and pepper
	2 wild ducks
Serves 4	4 fresh marjoram sprigs
Calories:	4 rashers of streaky bacon
466 per portion	

Peel the satsumas; separate the segments and remove all the pith. Put the satsuma segments into a pan with the chopped onion, orange juice, vermouth, stock and salt and pepper to taste; simmer gently for 5 minutes. Blend in the liquidizer until smooth.

Sprinkle the ducks inside and out with salt and pepper; put two sprigs of marjoram inside each bird. Stand them in a roasting tin, lay the bacon on the top. Cover the ducks with foil and roast in the oven for 45 minutes. Remove the foil and baste the ducks; return to the oven, uncovered, for about 15 minutes until just tender, but take care not to overcook.

Discard the bacon rashers. Cut off the leg joints from the duck neatly; carve the breasts into thin slices. Heat the satsuma sauce through gently. Serve the wild duck with the sauce spooned over one side.

180 PARTRIDGE WITH PEARS

Preparation time:	YOU WILL NEED:
30 minutes	1 sprig fresh rosemary
	2 bay leaves
Cooking time:	10 cloves
45-50 minutes	300 ml/½ pint dry white wine
Oven temperature:	300 ml/½ pint water
200°C, 400°F, gas 6	10 partridges
	salt
Serves 10	1 lemon, quartered
Calories:	10 firm pears, peeled
344 per portion	

Put the herbs and cloves in a saucepan with the wine and water, bring to the boil, cover and remove from the heat while you prepare the birds.

Rub each bird inside and out with salt and a cut lemon. Arrange them in two earthenware oven-to-table dishes, then arrange the pears around the birds.

Bring the wine mixture to the boil again quickly and pour over the birds and pears. Put in the oven. Cook for 45-50 minutes if both dishes fit on the centre shelf. If not, put the dishes on different shelves for 20 minutes, then swap them for the next 20 minutes. Change them over again for a further 15 minutes, then take the top dish out and keep it warm while you give the other dish a final 20 minutes in the centre of the oven. During cooking, check that the liquids do not dry up, topping up with more water if necessary. Serve one pear and a little of the cooking juice with each partridge.

■ COOK'S TIP

Satsumas have the great advantage of having no pips but they tend to have a lot of pith. If they are not available, you can use other members of the orange family such as mandarins or clementines.

■ COOK'S TIP

When choosing a partridge, look for yellow legs and sharp-pointed long wing feathers. Once the feathers are rounded, the bird is old and past its prime.

VEGETABLES & SALADS

The marvellous selection of vegetables available today means it is possible to create colourful, exciting salads and cooked vegetable dishes all the year round. Using herbs and spices in sauces and dressings enhances the subtle flavours of vegetables, while pulses provide valuable protein and fibre.

181 ORANGE WINTER SALAD

Preparation time:
20 minutes

Serves 4

Calories
278 per portion

YOU WILL NEED:
4 large oranges
1 x 400 g/14 oz can red kidney beans, drained
275 g/10 oz beansprouts
4 celery sticks, trimmed, scrubbed and thinly sliced
watercress sprigs, to garnish
FOR THE LIGHT FRENCH DRESSING
3 tablespoons olive oil
2 tablespoons lemon juice
salt
¼ teaspoon sugar
freshly ground black pepper
¼ teaspoon made English mustard

Using a serrated knife, cut the top and bottom from the oranges, then remove all the skin and pith, leaving a ball of fruit. Cut into segments by cutting down on either side of each membrane, and put in a bowl with any juice that runs out while cutting. Add the beans, beansprouts and celery and toss lightly together.

To make the dressing, put all the ingredients into a screw-topped jar and shake vigorously until blended.

Just before serving the salad spoon the dressing over and garnish with watercress.

182 MINTED COURGETTES WITH PEAS AND CORN

Preparation time:
5 minutes

Cooking time:
6-7 minutes

Serves 2

Calories:
53 per portion

YOU WILL NEED:
175 g/6 oz courgettes, thinly sliced
salt
50 g/2 oz frozen peas
50 g/2 oz frozen sweetcorn
2 mint sprigs
2 teaspoons chopped chives

Put the courgettes in a pan of boiling lightly salted water. Add the peas, sweetcorn and mint. Cover and simmer for 5-6 minutes until the vegetables are just tender. Drain, remove the mint and return the vegetables to the pan. Add the chives and toss to combine evenly.

Transfer to a warmed serving dish. Serve hot.

◼ COOK'S TIP

This crisp colourful salad is both delicious and nutritious. The watercress must be rinsed thoroughly in cold water and any discoloured leaves discarded.

◼ COOK'S TIP

Double the quantities of vegetables you are cooking for this dish and reserve half to include in a salad. If you are serving the courgettes with a low-calorie main course, try tossing the drained vegetables with a little butter.

183 BROAD BEANS WITH SESAME

Preparation time: 5-15 minutes	YOU WILL NEED: *450 g/1 lb broad beans, prepared weight, fresh or frozen*
Cooking time: 8-15 minutes	*2 tablespoons sesame seeds* *15 g/½ oz butter*
Serves 4	*1 tablespoon lemon juice* *freshly ground black pepper*
Calories: 191 per portion	

Cook the beans in boiling lightly salted water until tender, 8-15 minutes depending on whether fresh or frozen.

Meanwhile toast the sesame seeds under a moderate grill to brown them evenly.

Drain the beans, and put the butter in the pan. Melt it quickly and when just beginning to brown add the lemon juice and pepper. Tip the beans back into the pan and toss well in the butter.

Serve sprinkled with the sesame seeds.

184 LEMON CABBAGE WITH POPPY SEEDS

Preparation time: 15 minutes	YOU WILL NEED: *150 ml/¼ pint water* *salt*
Cooking time: 12 minutes	*350 g/12 oz green cabbage, shredded* *350 g/12 oz hard white cabbage, shredded*
Serves 4	*15 g/½ oz butter, cut into small pieces* *grated rind of 1 lemon*
Calories: 53 per portion	*1 ½ teaspoons poppy seeds* *freshly ground black pepper* *2 tablespoons smetana, to serve (optional)*

Put the water into a large saucepan, add a little salt and bring to the boil. Add both green and white cabbage, cover and simmer steadily for 7-10 minutes. The cabbage should be crisply tender and most of the water absorbed.

Take the lid off the pan and boil quickly to reduce any remaining liquid. Add the pieces of butter, lemon rind, poppy seeds and lots of black pepper. Stir briefly until the butter is melted and the cabbage evenly coated.

Spoon the hot cabbage into a warm dish and serve with smetana spooned over the top, if liked.

■ COOK'S TIP

Fresh broad bean pods may be a little discoloured. The actual beans inside can be perfect so do not discard without splitting the pod open to check.

■ COOK'S TIP

The colour contrast of the green and white cabbage gives this simple vegetable dish an attractive appearance. It can be served with meat or poultry dishes.

185 SPICY RED CABBAGE

Preparation time:
10 minutes

Cooking time:
8-12 minutes

Serves 4

Calories:
40 per portion

YOU WILL NEED:
1 medium red cabbage, shredded
1 tablespoon vinegar
2 teaspoons caraway seeds
¼ teaspoon ground allspice
1 tablespoon smetana
parsley sprig, to garnish

Rinse the cabbage under cold running water. Pour boiling water into a large saucepan to a depth of 1 cm/½ inch and add the cabbage, vinegar, caraway seeds and allspice.

Cover tightly and cook over a moderate heat for 8-12 minutes, stirring occasionally until the cabbage is tender.

Drain the cabbage thoroughly and transfer to a heated serving dish. Serve hot with the smetana spooned over the top, garnished with parsley.

186 SPICED CAULIFLOWER

Preparation time:
15 minutes

Cooking time:
15 minutes

Serves 4

Calories:
82 per portion

YOU WILL NEED:
1 tablespoon oil
·1 teaspoon ground ginger
2 teaspoons ground coriander
1 teaspoon ground turmeric
1 onion, sliced
1 cauliflower, broken into florets
2 carrots, thinly sliced
2 celery sticks, sliced
120 ml/4 fl oz stock
salt and pepper
150 ml/¼ pint natural low-fat yogurt
1 tablespoon chopped coriander or
    parsley

Heat the oil in a pan, add the spices and fry gently for 1 minute. Add the onion and cook gently for a further 3 minutes, stirring occasionally. Add the remaining vegetables, the stock, and salt and pepper to taste.

Cover and simmer for about 10 minutes until the vegetables are just tender. Stir in the yogurt, sprinkle with the coriander or parsley and serve immediately.

■ COOK'S TIP

Discard any limp outer leaves before shredding the red cabbage. Smetana is a low-fat substitute for cream with a slightly sour taste that also combines well with soft fruit. It is available in most supermarkets.

■ COOK'S TIP

Frying the spices gently brings out their flavour and aroma. Do not overcook the vegetables which should be quite crunchy. Use a chicken or vegetable stock.

187 SPINACH WITH YOGURT

Preparation time:
5-10 minutes

Cooking time:
5-10 minutes

Serves 4

Calories:
100 per portion

YOU WILL NEED:
1 kg/2¼ lb fresh spinach
150 ml/¼ pint natural low-fat yogurt
1-2 garlic cloves, crushed
salt and pepper

Rinse the spinach thoroughly in cold water and cook in a covered pan, without additional water, until tender. Shake the pan occasionally. Drain and leave to cool.

Mix together the yogurt and garlic and stir into the spinach. Add salt and pepper to taste. Transfer to a warmed serving dish.

188 MIXED VEGETABLE STIR-FRY

Preparation time:
20 minutes

Cooking time:
10 minutes

Serves 4

Calories:
124 per portion

YOU WILL NEED:
1 cauliflower, about 350 g/12 oz
2 carrots, about 100 g/4 oz
2 courgettes, about 175 g/6 oz
2 celery sticks
1 tablespoon vegetable oil
15 g/½ oz butter
2 tablespoons pumpkin seeds
salt and pepper

Break the cauliflower into very small florets. Cut the carrots into thin strips about 4 cm x 3 mm/1½ x ⅛ inch. Cut the courgettes into chunks, then into strips like the carrots. Trim the celery and cut into 4 cm/1½ inch lengths, then into strips in the same way.

Heat the oil and butter together in a large non-stick frying pan or wok. Add the pumpkin seeds and fry for about 1 minute, taking care as they will jump about in the heat.

Add all the vegetables at once, sprinkle with salt and pepper and cook over a steady heat, shaking the pan and turning the vegetables lightly for about 8-10 minutes until crisply tender. Serve immediately.

▨ COOK'S TIP

Frozen leaf spinach may be used if fresh spinach is not available. You will need 500 g/1¼ lb. Reserve the liquid to give flavour to a soup of leftover vegetables.

▨ COOK'S TIP

This is one of the best ways to cook vegetables. The colours stay bright and the quick cooking without water retains all the goodness. You can use other combinations of vegetables but always cut them in tiny pieces to ensure that they cook quickly and remain crisp.

189 STIR-FRIED CHINESE LEAVES

Preparation time:
15 minutes

Cooking time:
8 minutes

Serves 4

Calories:
82 per portion

YOU WILL NEED:
8-10 stems Chinese leaves
100 g/4 oz bamboo shoots, sliced
1 onion, sliced
1 celery stick, sliced
2 tablespoons oil
lemon juice
salt and pepper

Cut the Chinese leaves diagonally into 3 mm/⅛ inch strips.

Heat the oil in a non-stick frying pan or wok. Add the vegetables and fry gently for about 8 minutes, stirring frequently. Add a little lemon juice and seasoning to taste.

190 STIR-FRIED MUSHROOMS

Preparation time:
15 minutes

Cooking time:
7-8 minutes

Serves 4

Calories:
162 per portion

YOU WILL NEED:
225 g/8 oz mangetout, topped, tailed
   and cut diagonally into 4 cm/1 ½
   inch slices
salt
2 tablespoons vegetable oil
1 garlic clove, crushed
225 g/8 oz button mushrooms, sliced
25 g/1 oz cashew nuts
FOR THE SAUCE
2 tablespoons soy sauce
2 tablespoons dry sherry
5 tablespoons chicken stock
1 teaspoon clear honey
pinch of cayenne

Cook the mangetout slices in boiling lightly salted water for 2 minutes. Drain them, then plunge them immediately into ice cold water to prevent further cooking and to preserve their colour. Drain and dry with absorbent kitchen paper.

Mix all the sauce ingredients in a bowl.

Heat the oil in a heavy-based non-stick frying pan or wok and stir-fry the garlic with a pinch of salt over a high heat for 1 minute. Add the mangetout slices and the mushrooms and stir-fry them for 2 minutes.

Pour on the sauce, bring to the boil and cook for 2-3 minutes until the sauce has almost evaporated and the vegetables are just tender and glistening. Add the cashews and just heat through. Serve at once.

■ COOK'S TIP

If you only need a few drops of lemon juice, pierce the end of the fruit with a cocktail stick and squeeze gently.

■ COOK'S TIP

As their French name implies, the pods of mangetout peas are edible. They tend to be expensive: try growing some if you to have a garden.

191 STIR-FRIED GINGER BROCCOLI

Preparation time:
10 minutes

Cooking time:
3-4 minutes

Serves 4

Calories:
107 per portion

YOU WILL NEED:
500 g/1 ¼ lb broccoli
salt
2 tablespoons oil
1 garlic clove, thinly sliced (optional)
1 x 2.5 cm/1 inch piece fresh root ginger, finely shredded
½-1 teaspoon sesame oil

Separate the broccoli heads into small florets, and peel and diagonally slice the stems. Blanch in boiling lightly salted water for 30 seconds, drain well and cool rapidly under cold running water; drain thoroughly.

Heat the oil in a large non-stick frying pan or wok, add the garlic and ginger and stir-fry for 2-3 seconds. Add the blanched broccoli and cook for 2 minutes. Sprinkle over the sesame oil and stir fry for a further 30 seconds.

Spoon into a warmed serving dish and serve immediately.

192 VEGETABLES IN CURRY SAUCE

Preparation time:
20 minutes

Cooking time:
25 minutes

Serves 4

Calories:
180 per portion

YOU WILL NEED:
1 small cauliflower, cut into florets
225 g/8 oz carrots, thinly sliced
225 g/8 oz shelled broad beans
225 g/8 oz young French beans, topped, tailed and halved
450 ml/¾ pint vegetable stock
FOR THE SAUCE
1 tablespoon oil
1 small onion, chopped
2 teaspoons curry paste
1 tablespoon wholemeal flour
150 ml/¼ pint natural low-fat yogurt
1 teaspoon lemon juice
salt and pepper

Cook the vegetables in a covered steamer over the stock for 12 minutes, or simmer them in the stock for 9-10 minutes until they are just tender. Drain the vegetables and reserve the stock.

To make the sauce, heat the oil in a non-stick saucepan and fry the onion over a moderate heat for 3 minutes, stirring occasionally. Stir in the curry powder and curry paste and cook for 1 minute. Stir in the flour and cook for 2 minutes. Measure 275 ml/9 fl oz of the reserved stock and gradually pour it on to the curry mixture, stirring constantly. Gradually stir in the yogurt, then add the lemon juice and season with salt and pepper. Bring to the boil slowly and simmer for 2-3 minutes. Put the vegetables in a dish and stir in the sauce.

◾ COOK'S TIP

Garlic becomes quite mild and almost sweet in a slow-cooked casserole but if it is fried to a nutty brown, it is much more pungent.

◾ COOK'S TIP

Since the strict Hindu does not eat meat, much authentic Indian cooking is vegetarian. If you serve some plain boiled rice with these curried vegetables, *they will form a nutritious main course.*

193 INDIAN VEGETABLE MEDLEY

Preparation time:
20 minutes

Cooking time:
35 minutes

Serves 4

Calories:
142 per portion

YOU WILL NEED:
3 tablespoons oil
1 teaspoon fennel seeds
2 onions, sliced
1 teaspoon ground coriander
1 teaspoon cumin seeds
1 teaspoon chilli powder
2 teaspoons chopped root ginger
2 garlic cloves, crushed
1 small aubergine, thinly sliced
1 potato, cubed
1 green pepper, seeded and sliced
2 courgettes, sliced
1 x 400 g/14 oz can tomatoes
2 green chillies, chopped, including
   seeds
salt
50 g/2 oz frozen peas

Heat the oil in a large non-stick frying pan or wok, stir in the fennel seeds and cook for 1 minute, stirring constantly. Add the onion and cook for 5 minutes, until pale brown. Lower the heat, add all the spices and cook, stirring, for 1 minute. Add the ginger, garlic, aubergine and potato, mix well and cook for 15 minutes. Add the green pepper, courgettes, tomatoes with their juice, chillies and salt. Bring to the boil slowly and then simmer for 10 minutes, stirring occasionally.

Stir in the peas and cook for 3 minutes, until the vegetables are tender and the liquid absorbed.

■ COOK'S TIP

This vegetable medley has a fiery taste. Serve with natural low-fat yogurt for those who prefer milder flavours – and with a large jug of iced water!

194 GINGER DAL

Preparation time:
20 minutes

Cooking time:
1 hour

Serves 4

Calories:
222 per portion

YOU WILL NEED:
225 g/8 oz yellow split peas (see
   Cook's Tip)
600 ml/1 pint chicken or vegetable
   stock
175 g/6 oz cauliflower florets
1 tablespoon vegetable oil
½ teaspoon mustard seeds
½ teaspoon fennel seeds
1 teaspoon chopped root ginger
1 small onion, chopped
100 g/4 oz button mushrooms, thinly
   sliced
salt and pepper
FOR THE GARNISH
2 tablespoons chopped fresh coriander
   or parsley
lime slices
1 small onion, sliced into rings

Put the split peas and stock into a saucepan, bring to the boil, cover and simmer for about 45 minutes or until the split peas are tender. Meanwhile, steam the cauliflower florets for 10 minutes until they are beginning to soften.

Heat the oil in a small saucepan and fry the mustard, fennel seeds and ginger over a moderate heat for 1 minute, stirring. Add the onion and fry for 3-4 minutes, stirring. Add the onion mixture, the cauliflower and mushrooms to the pulses and season. Simmer for 5 minutes.

Turn the dal into a warmed dish. Sprinkle on the herb and arrange the lime slices and onion rings on top.

■ COOK'S TIP

Rinse the split peas thoroughly in cold water to remove any impurities and drain in a sieve before cooking. Unlike other pulses, neither lentils nor *split peas need to be soaked overnight.*

195 ORIENTAL VEGETABLES

Preparation time:
15 minutes

Cooking time:
20 minutes

Serves 4

Calories:
57 per portion

YOU WILL NEED:
450 g/1 lb mixed vegetables (see
   Cook's Tip)
120 ml/4 fl oz dry white wine
120 ml/4 fl oz wine vinegar
1 teaspoon coriander
1 teaspoon ground mace
1 teaspoon dried rosemary
salt

Put all the prepared vegetables in a suacepan with the white wine, vinegar, spices, rosemary and salt. Add enough water to cover, bring to the boil and simmer gently for 15-20 minutes. The vegetables should be slightly crisp. Serve hot or cold.

196 FENNEL IN WINE SAUCE

Preparation time:
10 minutes

Cooking time:
20-25 minutes

Serves 4

Calories:
138 per portion

YOU WILL NEED:
2-3 large heads fennel
2 teaspoons olive oil
2 garlic cloves, halved
300 ml/½ pint meat or vegetable stock
300 ml/½ pint dry white wine
3 tomatoes, cut into wedges
1 bay leaf
3 peppercorns
salt
sugar
pinch of curry powder
2 tablespoons coarsely chopped
   parsley
1 teaspoon cornflour

Remove the stalks from the fennel and cut the heads into quarters.

Heat the oil in a non-stick pan. Add the garlic and fry until golden brown. Remove and discard the garlic. Add the stock and wine to the pan, stirring well. Add the fennel, tomatoes, bay leaf and peppercorns. Season with salt and sugar to taste. Simmer over a low heat for 15-20 minutes. Add the curry powder and parsley, blending well. Discard the bay leaf.

Dissolve the cornflour in 2 teaspoons water. Add to the fennel mixture, stirring constantly. Cook, stirring, for 1-2 minutes. Transfer to a warmed serving dish and serve immediately.

■ COOK'S TIP

Try a mixture of cauliflower florets, onions cut into eighths, sliced leeks and sliced fennel. Try to combine vegetables which take a similar cooking time.

■ COOK'S TIP

Fennel with its slight taste of aniseed can also be cooked in a number of other ways which are suitable for celery or celeriac, such as braising or steaming whole. It is available throughout the winter.

197 PERSIAN NOODLES

Preparation time:
10 minutes, plus
draining

Cooking time:
16-20 minutes

Serves 4

Calories:
120 per portion

YOU WILL NEED:
1 large aubergine, thickly sliced
salt and pepper
600 ml/1 pint chicken stock
100 g/4 oz noodles
4 courgettes, sliced
1 teaspoon ground mace

Place the aubergine slices in a colander set over a plate, sprinkle with the salt and set aside to drain for 30 minutes.

Rinse the aubergine in cold water, drain and pat dry with absorbent kitchen paper, then chop into bite-sized pieces.

Place the stock in a large saucepan and bring to the boil. Add the noodles and cook for 5 minutes, then add the aubergine, courgettes, mace and pepper to taste.

Reduce the heat and cook for a further 10-15 minutes, or until the noodles and vegetables are tender. Adjust the seasoning to taste, drain and pile into a heated serving dish and serve.

198 BRAISED ONIONS IN CIDER AND SAGE

Preparation time:
10 minutes

Cooking time:
1¼ hours

Oven temperature:
180°C, 350°F, gas 4

Serves 4

Calories:
82 per portion

YOU WILL NEED:
2 large Spanish onions, about 450 g/
   1lb total weight
1 tablespoon vegetable oil
300 ml/½ pint dry cider
salt and pepper
2 teaspoons chopped fresh sage or ½
   teaspoon dried sage
1 teaspoon cornflour
1 tablespoon water

Remove the papery skins from the onions and cut each into quarters. Trim the bases very lightly so that the quarters stay intact during cooking. Heat the oil in a non-stick frying pan and quickly fry the onion quarters on all sides until golden brown. Put the onions in a small shallow casserole, cut side up. Pour the cider into the pan with the salt, pepper and sage. Bring to the boil, then pour over the onions. Cover the casserole and cook in the oven for 40 minutes.

Remove from the oven, blend the cornflour with the water and stir into the liquor surrounding the onions. Cover again and replace in the oven for a further 20 minutes, by which time the onions will be tender and the sauce slightly thickened. Serve hot.

■ COOK'S TIP

Mace comes from the nutmeg: it is, in fact, the net-like covering on the nutmeg. It is used either whole or ground to a fine powder.

■ COOK'S TIP

Vegetables cooked in their own sauce like these braised onions are ideal for serving with any lean meat or poultry. You will not need to make any gravy.

199 STUFFED SPANISH ONIONS

Preparation time:	**YOU WILL NEED:**
20 minutes	*2 large Spanish onions, halved*
	salt and pepper
Cooking time:	*15 g/½ oz butter*
40 minutes	*50 g/2 oz lean smoked bacon,*
	derinded and chopped
Oven temperature:	*3 tomatoes, peeled and chopped*
220°C, 425°F, gas 7	*150 g/5 oz button mushrooms, sliced*
	1 tablespoon chopped parsley
Serves 4	*1 tablespoon grated Parmesan cheese*
Calories:	*1-2 teaspoons dried oregano*
107 per portion	

Scoop a hollow in the centre of each onion half with a tea-spoon, reserving the scooped out onion. Place the halves in a saucepan and cover with water. Add a little salt, bring to the boil and cook for about 15 minutes, until almost tender. Drain well.

Meanwhile, chop the reserved onion. Melt the butter in a non-stick frying pan and cook the bacon and onion for 4-5 minutes. Add the tomatoes and mushrooms and cook for a further 2-3 minutes. Remove the pan from the heat, stir in the parsley and cheese and season to taste with salt, pepper and oregano.

Fill the onion halves with this mixture and put in an oven-proof dish. Cover the base of the dish with water to a depth of 1 cm/½ inch. Cook in the oven for 12-15 minutes.

200 CELERIAC STICKS WITH MUSTARD

Preparation time:	**YOU WILL NEED:**
15 minutes	*750 g/1½ lb celeriac*
	salt
Cooking time:	*1 tablespoon lemon juice*
25 minutes	*FOR THE DRESSING*
Serves 6	*150 ml/¼ pint natural low-fat yogurt*
	freshly ground black pepper
Calories:	*1 tablespoon wholegrain mustard*
62 per portion	*FOR THE GARNISH*
	lemon slices
	coriander leaves or parsley sprigs

Peel the celeriac and cut first into thick slices, then into chips about 7.5 x 1 cm/3 x ½ inch. Put the chips into a pan with a pinch of salt and the lemon juice and cover with water. Bring to the boil, cover the pan and simmer for 15-20 minutes until the celeriac is tender but still firm. Drain and keep warm in a serving dish.

Pour the yogurt into the rinsed-out pan and stir in the salt, pepper and mustard. Heat very gently until hot, taking care that it does not boil. Pour the cream and mustard dressing over the celeriac and garnish with lemon slices and the cor-iander leaves or parsley. Serve immediately.

■ COOK'S TIP

Check the onions for tenderness after they have been boiled for about 15 minutes. The time will, of course, depend on how much onion you have scooped out from the centres.

■ COOK'S TIP

Celeriac looks rather like a knobbly swede. It tastes rather like celery and it has a texture rather like a turnip. It can also be served cold with French dressing.

201 CHICKEN LIVER AND WALNUT SALAD

Preparation time:
15 minutes

Cooking time:
10 minutes

Serves 4

Calories:
254 per portion

YOU WILL NEED:
5 teaspoons walnut or olive oil
450 g/1 lb chicken livers
25 g/1 oz walnut pieces
1 garlic clove, crushed (optional)
2 teaspoons wine vinegar
3 tablespoons natural low-fat yogurt
salt and pepper
½ lettuce, washed and torn into pieces
50 g/2 oz radishes, trimmed and very
  thinly sliced
4 spring onions, trimmed and finely
  chopped

Brush a thick saucepan with 1 teaspoon of the oil and heat gently. With kitchen scissors snip the chicken livers into quarters, directly into the pan, cutting off and discarding any green parts. Stir over a medium heat for 4 minutes. Add the walnut pieces, turn the heat down as low as possible, cover tightly and simmer for a further 5 minutes. The livers should be just cooked and still slightly pink inside.

Meanwhile, blend the remaining oil with the garlic (if using), vinegar, yogurt, salt and pepper in a jug. Place the lettuce, radishes and spring onions in a bowl and toss.

Divide the vegetable mixture among four shallow bowls or dinner plates. Spoon the liver quarters with the walnuts and pan juices over the vegetables and serve, accompanied by the dressing.

■ COOK'S TIP

Although walnut oil is expensive, it is well worth using it rather than olive oil to give the authentic flavour to this unusual warm salad. The juices from the chicken liver combine deliciously with the crunchy vegetables.

202 GAZPACHO RING

Preparation time:
20 minutes, plus
chilling

Cooking time:
8 minutes

Serves 6

Calories:
43 per portion

YOU WILL NEED:
1 x 400 g/14 oz can tomatoes
2 garlic cloves, chopped
150 ml/¼ pint water
bouquet garni (see Recipe 109)
salt and pepper
1 tablespoon powdered gelatine
4 tablespoons water
2 tablespoons light French dressing
  (see Recipe 181)
FOR THE SALAD
4 tomatoes, peeled, seeded and diced
¼ cucumber, diced
½ green pepper, seeded and diced
½ onion, finely chopped

Put the tomatoes, with their juice, in a saucepan with the garlic, water and bouquet garni. Add salt and pepper to taste. Bring slowly to the boil, then simmer for 5 minutes. Discard the bouquet garni.

Dissolve the gelatine with the water in a small bowl over a pan of gently simmering water.

Put the tomato mixture in a blender or food processor. Add the gelatine and blend on maximum speed for 30 seconds. Leave to cool.

Add half the salad ingredients and stir well. Turn into a 750 ml/1 ¼ pint non-stick ring mould and chill for about 3 hours, or until set. Mix the remaining salad ingredients with the French dressing. Turn out the tomato ring on to a serving plate and place the salad in the centre.

■ COOK'S TIP

In the centre of the gazpacho ring, add some lean chopped chicken or white fish to make a main course dish and accompany with a crisp green salad.

203 SWEDISH CUCUMBER SALAD

Preparation time:
10 minutes, plus
draining

Serves 6

Calories:
28 per portion

YOU WILL NEED:
1 cucumber
salt
FOR THE DRESSING
1 tablespoon clear honey
1 tablespoon water
2 tablespoons chopped dill or fennel
4 tablespoons white wine vinegar

Slice the cucumber very thinly and place in a colander. Sprinkle liberally with salt and leave to drain for 30 minutes.

Meanwhile, mix the dressing ingredients together in a screw-topped jar. Shake well and leave for 30 minutes.

Dry the cucumber thoroughly on absorbent kitchen paper. Arrange the cucumber slices overlapping in a shallow dish and pour over the dressing.

204 ROMAN RED CABBAGE SALAD

Preparation time:
15 minutes, plus
standing

Cooking time:
5 minutes

Serves 4

Calories:
138 per portion

YOU WILL NEED:
3 teaspoons lemon juice
2 bananas, peeled and sliced
1 apple, cored and sliced
1 medium red cabbage, shredded
15 g/½ oz walnut halves
2 tablespoons red wine vinegar
2 teaspoons honey
salt and pepper

Sprinkle the lemon juice over the banana and apple slices to prevent discoloration. Mix the cabbage with the banana, apple and walnuts in a serving bowl.

To make the dressing, heat the vinegar in a small pan until warm and add the honey, stirring well to dissolve. Season with salt and pepper to taste. Leave until cool.

Pour the dressing over the red cabbage mixture, and toss well. Leave the salad to stand for a few minutes before serving to allow the flavours to develop.

■ COOK'S TIP

Cucumber salad is the perfect choice to serve with either hot or cold fish. The addition of either dill or fennel also makes the dressing particularly *suitable as an accompaniment to a fish dish.*

■ COOK'S TIP

This salad is particularly good served with pheasant. Red cabbage is easily obtainable during winter and is far less expensive than green salad leaves.

205 MIXED BEAN AND CORN SALAD

Preparation time:
15 minutes, plus
soaking and
standing

Cooking time:
45 minutes

Serves 4

Calories:
221 per portion

YOU WILL NEED:
75 g/3 oz red kidney beans, soaked
   overnight
75 g/3 oz haricot beans, soaked
   overnight
75 g/3 oz fresh or frozen green beans
1 x 200 g/7 oz can sweetcorn, drained
1 tablespoon chopped mixed herbs or
   2 teaspoons dried herbs
4 tablespoons light French dressing
   (see Recipe 181)

Drain the kidney and haricot beans, rinse and place in separate pans. Cover the cold water and bring to the boil. Cook rapidly for 10 minutes, then reduce the heat and cook for 30-35 minutes, or until the beans are tender. Drain and place in a serving bowl.

Cook the green and broad beans in boiling water until tender, then drain and add to the serving bowl. Stir in the sweetcorn and herbs. Pour the French dressing over the salad, then mix well. If possible, add the dressing while the beans are still warm and leave at room temperature for 1-2 hours before serving.

206 SAVOY SALAD

Preparation time:
15 minutes

Cooking time:
2 minutes

Serves 4

Calories:
114 per portion

YOU WILL NEED:
1 teaspoon caraway seeds
2 tablespoons olive or sunflower oil
2 teaspoons lemon juice
1 teaspoon red wine vinegar
1 teaspoon mild mustard
pinch of pepper
pinch of salt
100 g/4 oz cottage or smooth low-fat
   soft cheese
2 tablespoons water
225 g/8 oz Savoy cabbage, very finely
   shredded
100 g/4 oz red or green pepper, seeded
   and finely diced

Put the caraway seeds in an ungreased heavy-based frying pan and stir over a low heat for 1-2 minutes. Crush in an electric coffee mill or with a mortar and pestle.

Transfer to a blender and add the oil, lemon juice, vinegar, mustard, pepper, salt, cheese and water. Blend the dressing until smooth.

Place the prepared cabbage and pepper in a serving bowl and stir well. Spoon the dressing over and serve.

207 SPRING CABBAGE AND PEPPER SALAD

Preparation time:	YOU WILL NEED:
15 minutes, plus marinating	*250 g/9 oz spring cabbage, shredded*
	4 tablespoons light French dressing (see Recipe 181)
Serves 6	*1 teaspoon light soy sauce*
Calories:	*3 celery sticks, sliced*
57 per portion	*4 spring onions, chopped*
	1 red pepper, seeded and diced

Combine the dressing with the soy sauce. Put the spring cabbage in a bowl with the dressing, toss thoroughly and leave to marinate for 1 hour.

Add the remaining ingredients and toss thoroughly. Transfer to a salad bowl to serve.

208 CHARLOTTE D'AUBERGINES

Preparation time:	YOU WILL NEED:
20 minutes, plus standing	*1 kg/2¼ lb aubergines, sliced*
	salt
Cooking time:	*15 g/½ oz butter*
1½ hours	*1 large onion, sliced*
	2 garlic cloves, crushed
Oven temperature:	*500 g/1¼ lb tomatoes, peeled and chopped*
180°C, 350°F, gas 4	*2 tablespoons oil*
Serves 6	*300 ml/½ pint natural low-fat yogurt*
Calories:	*150 ml/¼ pint chicken stock*
122 per portion	

Sprinkle the aubergine slices with salt and leave to stand for 30 minutes. Rinse under cold water and dry thoroughly with absorbent kitchen paper.

Melt the butter in a non-stick frying pan, add the onion and garlic and fry until lightly browned. Stir in the tomatoes and cook for 20-25 minutes, until thickened.

Heat the oil in another non-stick pan and fry the aubergine slices until browned on both sides. Drain thoroughly on absorbent kitchen paper.

Line the base and sides of a 1.5 litre/2 ½ pint charlotte mould with aubergine slices. Fill with layers of the tomato mixture, yogurt and aubergines, finishing with aubergines. Cover with foil and cook in the oven for 40-45 minutes, until tender. Leave for 10 minutes, then turn out on to a warmed serving dish. Heat any remaining tomato sauce with the stock and spoon around the charlotte.

■ COOK'S TIP

Spring cabbage is an unusual ingredient for a salad. Pick over the leaves carefully, discarding any that are blemished. Make this salad the same day as you obtain the spring cabbage as the leaves soon become limp.

■ COOK'S TIP

Sliced or halved aubergines should always be sprinkled with salt and left to stand as this will draw out the bitter juices.

209 SPRING GREEN SALAD

Preparation time:
15 minutes, plus
marinating

Serves 6

Calories:
94 per portion

YOU WILL NEED:
225 g/8 oz spring greens
3 tablespoons olive oil
2 teaspoons soy sauce
1 tablespoon lemon juice
2 garlic cloves, crushed
salt and pepper
3 celery sticks
½ x 200 g/7 oz can sweetcorn,
    drained
2 tablespoons chopped parsley

Shred the spring greens finely and place in a mixing bowl. Mix together the oil, soy sauce, lemon juice, garlic, and salt and pepper to taste and pour over the greens. Mix thoroughly and leave to marinate for 1 hour.

Slice the celery and add to the salad with the sweetcorn and parsley. Mix thoroughly, then transfer to a serving dish.

210 CRISP WINTER SALAD

Preparation time:
10 minutes

Cooking time:
3 minutes

Serves 4

Calories:
64 per portion

YOU WILL NEED:
40 g/1½ oz flaked almonds
225 g/8 oz celery, thinly sliced
1 large orange, about 175 g/6 oz flesh,
    peeled, segmented and roughly
    chopped
150 ml/¼ pint natural low-fat yogurt
1 teaspoon ground coriander
    (optional)
½ teaspoon ground cumin or fennel
    seeds
pinch of salt (optional)

Place the almonds in an ungreased heavy-based frying pan over a low heat for 2-3 minutes, stirring until slightly browned.

Put half the almonds with the prepared celery and orange in a serving bowl and toss lightly.

Combine the yogurt, coriander (if using) and cumin or fennel seeds. Pour over the salad. Taste and add a little salt if necessary. Sprinkle the remaining almonds over the salad and serve.

■ COOK'S TIP

Some people still associate salads with summer meals but equally appetizing mixtures can also be prepared in winter.

■ COOK'S TIP

The crunchy combination of textures, sweetened with orange and spices, makes this salad a good addition to a winter menu. The yogurt blends perfectly with the orange to form a refreshing dressing.

211 POIREAUX VINAIGRETTE

Preparation time:
15 minutes, plus
chilling

Serves 4

Calories:
133 per portion

YOU WILL NEED:
6 *leeks*
1 *tablespoon chopped capers*
FOR THE DRESSING
2 *tablespoons lemon juice*
3 *tablespoons olive oil*
1 *teaspoon Meaux mustard*
1 *garlic clove, crushed*
salt and pepper
1 *tablespoon chopped parsley*
1 *tablespoon chopped chives*

Slice the leeks very finely and arrange in a salad bowl.

Put the dressing ingredients in a screw-topped jar and shake well. Pour over the leeks, add the capers and toss well. Chill for 1 hour before serving.

212 TROPICAL SALAD

Preparation time:
15 minutes

Serves 4

Calories:
357 per portion

YOU WILL NEED:
275 *g/10 oz long-grain brown rice,*
  cooked
50 *g/2 oz dried coconut flakes*
½ *cucumber, unpeeled and cut into 1*
  cm/½ inch cubes
1 *small ripe pineapple, peeled, cored*
  and cut into 2.5 cm/1 inch pieces
1 *tablespoon olive oil*
1 *teaspoon lemon juice*
salt and pepper
FOR THE GARNISH
50 *g/2 oz whole blanched almonds,*
  toasted
pineapple leaves

Put the rice, coconut, cucumber and pineapple into a bowl. Add the oil and lemon juice and a little salt and pepper, taste and adjust the seasoning if necessary, then spoon into a serving dish.

Scatter the almonds over the salad and garnish with the pineapple leaves.

■ COOK'S TIP

A good juicy lemon should yield about 3 tablespoons of juice. If you first warm the lemon in a cool oven, it will produce more juice. Try using other types of mustard *in the dressing as a variation.*

■ COOK'S TIP

If coconut flakes are not available, use unsweetened desiccated coconut. Replace fresh pineapple with a 400-g/14-oz can of pineapple in natural juice.

213 MUSHROOM SALAD

Preparation time:
15 minutes, plus
standing

Serves 4

Calories:
108 per portion

YOU WILL NEED:
250 g/9 oz button mushrooms
juice of ½ lemon
2 tablespoons sliced gherkins
175 g/6 oz tomatoes, finely chopped
1 garlic clove, crushed with salt
1 parsley sprig, finely chopped
freshly ground black pepper
pinch of sugar
3 tablespoons olive oil

Trim the mushroom stalks level with the caps. Put into a sieve, rinse and drain thoroughly. Cut into thin slices, put into a bowl and sprinkle with the lemon juice. Add the gherkins and tomatoes and mix well to blend.

To make the dressing, beat the garlic with the parsley, pepper to taste, sugar and oil. Pour over the mushroom salad and toss well to mix. Leave to marinate in the refrigerator for 10-15 minutes to allow the flavours to develop. Serve lightly chilled.

214 RADICCHIO WITH GARLIC DRESSING

Preparation time:
10 minutes, plus
standing

Serves 6

Calories:
68 per portion

YOU WILL NEED:
2 heads of radicchio
3 garlic cloves, finely chopped
1 tablespoon shredded basil leaves
salt and pepper
1 teaspoon grated Parmesan cheese
3 tablespoons olive oil
1 tablespoon wine vinegar

Remove the outer leaves from the radicchio and cut away the thick stems. Separate the leaves, tearing the larger leaves into pieces. Put in a sieve, rinse and drain thoroughly. Arrange in a salad bowl.

To make the dressing, beat the garlic with the basil, salt and pepper to taste, cheese, oil and vinegar. Pour over the radicchio and toss lightly. Leave to stand for a few minutes before serving to allow the flavours to develop.

■ COOK'S TIP

This piquant salad makes a delicious accompaniment to cold roast chicken. It can also be served as a starter or packed into a lidded plastic box for a picnic.

■ COOK'S TIP

This is a delicious simple salad which can be served as a starter or as an accompaniment. In Italy it is often eaten with plainly cooked veal escalopes.

215 RED AND GREEN SALAD

Preparation time:
25 minutes, plus
standing

Serves 4

Calories:
220 per portion

YOU WILL NEED:
225 g/8 oz courgettes, sliced
100 g/4 oz button mushrooms, thinly
  sliced
2 tablespoons snipped fresh chives
4 large tomatoes, thinly sliced
½ cucumber, thinly sliced
1 red pepper, seeded and thinly sliced
  into rings
FOR THE DRESSING
4 tablespoons vegetable oil
2 tablespoons red wine vinegar
salt and pepper
pinch of mustard powder
5 tablespoons buttermilk, or natural
  low-fat yogurt
15 g/½ oz blue cheese, crumbled
50 g/2 oz Ricotta cheese, crumbled

Mix together the oil, vinegar, salt, pepper and mustard. Put
the courgettes and the mushrooms in separate dishes and
divide the dressing between them. Stir the chives into the
courgettes. Set aside for at least 1 hour.

Arrange the tomatoes, cucumber and pepper in rings on a
dish. Drain the courgettes, reserving the dressing, and make a
ring with them. Drain the mushrooms, reserving the dressing,
and arrange them in the centre.

Stir the buttermilk or yogurt into the dressing and stir in the
cheeses. Spoon into the centre of the salad.

216 CAULIFLOWER AND MUSHROOM SALAD

Preparation time:
15 minutes, plus
cooling

Cooking time:
5 minutes

Serves 8

Calories:
83 per portion

YOU WILL NEED:
250 g/9 oz cauliflower, broken into
  florets
100 g/4 oz button mushrooms, sliced
1 avocado, halved, stoned, peeled and
  sliced
25 g/1 oz flaked almonds, toasted
FOR THE DRESSING
150 ml/¼ pint natural low-fat yogurt
1 teaspoon lemon juice
1 garlic clove, crushed
paprika
chopped chives

Cook the cauliflower in boiling, salted water for 2 minutes;
drain and leave to cool completely. Place in a bowl with the
mushrooms, avocado and almonds.

Mix the dressing ingredients together, adding salt and
paprika to taste. Pour over the vegetables and toss
thoroughly. Transfer to a serving dish and sprinkle with the
chives.

▨ COOK'S TIP

*Ricotta is a low-fat Italian
cheese which is made from
the whey, not the curds, of
cow's or goat's milk. It can
be bought as a soft cheese
or in a hardened form.*

▨ COOK'S TIP

*Avocados are high in
calories so slimmers should
not combine them with any
dressing containing oil.
Their creamy texture blends
well with the cauliflower.*

217 MUSHROOM, COURGETTE AND TOMATO SALAD

Preparation time:
15 minutes

Serves 4

Calories:
74 per portion

YOU WILL NEED:
6 large mushrooms, sliced
4 courgettes, thinly sliced
4 tomatoes, peeled and quartered
1 teaspoon chopped fresh basil
1 bunch of cress, trimmed and divided
    into sprigs
3 tablespoons light French dressing
    (see Recipe 181)

Combine the mushrooms, courgettes and tomatoes in a salad bowl and sprinkle with the basil.

Arrange the sprigs of cress round the edge of the salad. Serve with the light French dressing.

218 CHINESE SALAD

Preparation time:
15 minutes

Serves 4

Calories:
39 per portion

YOU WILL NEED:
175 g/6 oz red cabbage, finely
    shredded
few Chinese leaves, shredded
100 g/4 oz bean sprouts, rinsed
2 celery sticks, chopped
5 cm/2 inch piece of cucumber, cut
    into strips
FOR THE DRESSING
4 tablespoons natural low-fat yogurt
1 teaspoons soy sauce
salt and pepper

Put the red cabbage in a bowl and add the Chinese leaves, bean sprouts, celery and cucumber.

Mix together the dressing ingredients, with salt and pepper to taste, and add to the vegetables. Mix well and transfer to a serving bowl.

■ COOK'S TIP

A combination of contrasting colours gives a salad visual appeal. Mushrooms, courgettes and tomatoes not only look good together, they also complement each other in taste. The salad could be bordered with watercress.

■ COOK'S TIP

The addition of soy sauce gives a piquancy to the dressing. The Chinese leaves add both colour contrast and a crunchy texture to the salad.

219 RED AND WHITE SALAD

Preparation time:
15 minutes

Cooking time:
50 minutes

Serves 4

Calories:
88 per portion

YOU WILL NEED:
225 g/8 oz fresh beetroot, scrubbed
225 g/8 oz eating apple, washed
about 2 tablespoons lemon juice
2 chicory heads, cut into 1 cm/ ½ inch
thick slices
150 ml/¼ pint natural low-fat yogurt
or cultured buttermilk
¼ teaspoon pepper
½-1 teaspoon mild mustard
pinch of salt
2 teaspoons sunflower oil

Boil or steam the beetroot for about 50 minutes until tender. Drain and dice.

Quarter and core the apple, then cut into small cubes. Toss in the lemon juice immediately to avoid discoloration. Mix the apple with the chicory in a serving dish. Combine the yogurt or buttermilk, pepper, mustard, salt and oil in a jug. Spoon over the salad. Stir in the beetroot just before serving, as its colour will quickly stain the other salad ingredients.

220 COURGETTE AND RADICCHIO SALAD

Preparation time:
15 minutes, plus
standing

Serves 6

Calories:
95 per portion

YOU WILL NEED:
4 tablespoons light French dressing
(see Recipe 181)
1 garlic clove, crushed
250 g/9 oz courgettes, thinly sliced
1 head of radicchio
50 g/2 oz black olives, halved and
stoned
1 tablespoon pine nuts
salt and pepper

Put the French dressing and garlic in a salad bowl. Add the sliced courgettes and toss well. Leave to stand for 30 minutes to allow the courgettes to absorb the flavour of the dressing.

Tear the radicchio leaves into manageable pieces and add to the courgettes and dressing with the black olives and pine nuts. Season with salt and pepper to taste. Toss the salad thoroughly before serving.

■ COOK'S TIP

Cultured buttermilk is available in the dairy section of many large supermarkets. Sunflower oil is a useful all-purpose oil with a milder flavour than *olive oil. Diced Chinese leaves may be used instead of the chicory.*

■ COOK'S TIP

Pine nuts are an important ingredient of vegetarian cooking. They are high in protein. They have long been used in Italian and French dishes.

221 EGG AND CUCUMBER SALAD

Preparation time:
20 minutes

Serves 4

Calories:
143 per portion

YOU WILL NEED:
1 bunch of watercress
1 cucumber, peeled and sliced
4 hard-boiled eggs, finely chopped
1 bunch of spring onions, chopped
FOR THE SAUCE
300 ml/½ pint natural low-fat yogurt
1 tablespoon lemon juice
1 teaspoon mustard powder
salt and pepper

Arrange the watercress in a serving dish and cover with the cucumber slices. Mix the chopped eggs and spring onions together and spoon into the centre.

To make the sauce, mix all the ingredients together. Pour over the salad and serve.

222 TOMATO RING SALAD

Preparation time:
15 minutes, plus setting

Cooking time:
5 minutes

Serves 4

Calories:
63 per portion

YOU WILL NEED:
4 tomatoes, skinned and sliced
600 ml/1 pint tomato juice
1 teaspoon Worcestershire sauce
salt and pepper
15 g/½ oz powdered gelatine
3 tablespoons water
FOR THE GARNISH
endive leaves
watercress sprigs

Arrange the tomato slices in the base of a 900 ml/1½ pint ring mould. Pour the tomato juice into a small saucepan and bring to the boil. Reduce the heat and stir in the Worcestershire sauce with salt and pepper to taste.

Dissolve the gelatine with the water in a small bowl over a pan of gently simmering water. Combine with the tomato juice and pour into the mould. Allow to cool, then chill in the refrigerator for 3 hours, or until set.

To serve, dip the mould into hot water for a few seconds, then place a serving plate on top of the mould and invert with a sharp shake to unmould it. Fill the centre of the mould with endive leaves, top with watercress and serve chilled.

■ COOK'S TIP

To avoid a black rim forming around the yolks of hard-boiled eggs, cook them for a maximum of 9 minutes and plunge into cold water immediately, *tapping the shells as you do so. If you use a wet knife to slice hard-boiled eggs, the yolks will not crumble as you cut them.*

■ COOK'S TIP

For a complete light meal, fill the centre of the mould with cottage cheese mixed with finely chopped spring onion and fresh basil.

223 CHICK PEA SALAD

Preparation time:
10 minutes, plus
soaking and cooling

Cooking time:
1½-2 hours

Serves 6

Calories:
180 per portion

YOU WILL NEED:
250 g/9 oz chick peas, soaked
*   overnight*
salt
4 tablespoons light French dressing
*   (see Recipe 181)*
½ teaspoon ground ginger
1 small onion, chopped
1 red pepper, seeded and diced
2 tablespoons chopped parsley

Drain the chick peas, put in a saucepan and cover with cold water. Bring to the boil and simmer for 1½-2 hours or until softened, adding a little salt towards the end of cooking.

Drain thoroughly and place in a bowl. Blend the French dressing with the ground ginger. Pour over the dressing and toss well while still warm. Leave to cool.

Add the remaining ingredients, toss thoroughly and transfer to a serving dish.

224 PASTA AND BEAN SALAD

Preparation time:
15 minutes, plus
cooling

Cooking time:
8-10 minutes

Serves 4

Calories:
231 per portion

YOU WILL NEED:
2 tablespoons olive oil
3 tablespoons unsweetened orange juice
1 garlic clove, crushed
salt and pepper
2 tablespoons finely chopped parsley
175 g/6 oz wholemeal pasta shapes
175 g/6 oz cooked red kidney beans
50 g/2 oz soya bean sprouts
2 tablespoons natural low-fat yogurt
1 tablespoon chopped chives
75 g/3 oz alfalfa salad sprouts

Mix the olive oil with the orange juice, garlic, salt and pepper to taste and the chopped parsley.

Cook the wholemeal pasta shapes in a large pan of boiling salted water until tender (8-10 minutes, depending on the size of the pasta shapes). Drain the pasta shapes thoroughly and stir into the orange and oil dressing while the pasta is still warm. Allow to cool.

Mix in the kidney beans and soya bean sprouts; stir in the yogurt and chives. Spoon the prepared salad on to a shallow serving dish and arrange the alfalfa salad sprouts around the edge. Serve as a complete light meal.

▨ COOK'S TIP

Although chick peas are
also available canned, it is
worth the effort of soaking
the dried variety overnight
as you then know no
preservatives have been used.

▨ COOK'S TIP

To sprout soya beans: soak 2
tablespoons of beans
overnight, drain and put in a
clean jar. Fill with water and
leave 4 days, changing the
water daily.

225 SALADE NICOISE

Preparation time:
20 minutes

Serves 6

Calories:
165 per portion

YOU WILL NEED:
⅓ crisp lettuce
3 eggs, hard-boiled
1 x 400 g/14 oz can artichoke hearts
1 x 200 g/7 oz can tuna fish in brine, drained
1 x 50 g/2 oz can anchovy fillets, drained
250 g/9 oz tomatoes, peeled and quartered
150 g/5 oz French beans, cooked
8-10 black olives, stoned
1-2 teaspoons capers
1 tablespoon chopped parsley
4 tablespoons light French dressing (see Recipe 181)

Line a serving bowl with the lettuce.

Cut the eggs into quarters. Drain the artichoke hearts, tuna and anchovy fillets and arrange in the prepared bowl, together with the remaining salad ingredients.

Put the dressing ingredients in a screw-topped jar and shake well. Pour over the salad, toss well and serve immediately.

226 PASTA, CUCUMBER AND RADISH SALAD

Preparation time:
20 minutes

Cooking time:
10 minutes

Serves 4

Calories:
113 per portion

YOU WILL NEED:
100 g/4 oz pasta shapes
salt
175 g/6 oz radishes, trimmed, washed and sliced
½ cucumber, about 225 g/8 oz, unpeeled and diced
150 ml/¼ pint natural low-fat yogurt
freshly ground black pepper
1 cos lettuce, washed and dried
2 spring onions, trimmed, peeled and finely chopped, to garnish

Put the pasta into a large pan of boiling lightly salted water. Bring back to the boil and cook for about 10 minutes until 'al dente'. Rinse under cold running water and drain thoroughly.

Put the radishes and cucumber into a bowl and add the pasta. Stir in the yogurt adding plenty of black pepper and a little salt. Turn the pasta, radishes and cucumber over in the yogurt to coat thoroughly.

Arrange the lettuce leaves on a serving dish and spoon the salad into them. Garnish with the chopped spring onions.

▨ COOK'S TIP

Every cook along the Provençal coast has his or her own family recipe for Salade Niçoise. The locally caught tuna and anchovies are invariably included with the glossy black olives which grow in abundance.

▨ COOK'S TIP

For this main course salad, it is best not to peel the cucumber as its green skin looks so decorative. Choose from a wide variety of pasta shapes.

227 WATERCRESS WITH ORANGE AND NUTS

Preparation time:
15 minutes, plus
standing

Serves 4

Calories:
63 per portion

YOU WILL NEED:
1 bunch of watercress
1 large orange
1 tablespoon chopped hazelnuts
120 ml/4 fl oz natural low-fat yogurt
½ garlic clove, crushed with salt
pinch of sugar
2 teaspoons chopped parsley
freshly ground black pepper

Trim the watercress stems, sort the leaves, put in a sieve, rinse and drain thoroughly. Put in a large serving bowl.

Peel and segment the orange, removing all pith, then chop roughly. Add the orange and hazelnuts to the watercress.

To make the piquant dressing beat the yogurt with the garlic, sugar, parsley and pepper to taste. Pour over the watercress and toss well. Leave to stand for about 30 minutes before serving to allow the flavours to blend and develop.

228 SPINACH WITH FLAKED ALMONDS

Preparation time:
15 minutes

Cooking time:
15-20 minutes

Serves 4

Calories:
132 per portion

YOU WILL NEED:
1 kg/2¼ lb leaf spinach
15 g/½ oz butter
½ onion, finely chopped
salt
grated nutmeg
3 tablespoons natural low-fat yogurt
40 g/1½ oz flaked almonds

Sort the spinach, put in a sieve, rinse and drain thoroughly. Tear the leaves into manageable pieces.

Melt the butter in a large pan, add the onion and cook for 2-3 minutes until softened. Add the spinach, a little at a time, turning it in the butter to coat. Season with salt and nutmeg to taste. Cover and cook over a low heat for 10-15 minutes, until tender, depending upon the thickness of the spinach leaves.

Stir the yogurt into the spinach mixture. Immediately remove the spinach from the heat and transfer to a warmed serving bowl. Add the flaked almonds to the butter remaining in the pan and fry, stirring, until golden. Fold the almonds into the spinach and serve immediately.

▨ COOK'S TIP

An attractive way of serving this salad as a starter is to fill the mixture into grapefruit or orange shells, especially if you first vandyke the edges.

▨ COOK'S TIP

Other members of the spinach family such as spinach beet or orache may be cooked in the same way.

DESSERTS

The dessert course, usually high in calories, often proves an irresistible temptation to weight-watchers. The recipes in this chapter show how favourite desserts including fools and ice creams can still be enjoyed. Fruit is the obvious choice as a base for low-calorie desserts. Visually appealing and naturally sweet, it can be combined with other ingredients to make both hot and cold desserts. Natural low-fat yogurt or sometimes smetana is used instead of cream in these recipes.

229 SPICED PEARS

Preparation time:
20 minutes, plus cooling

Cooking time:
15-20 minutes

Serves 4

Calories:
111 per portion

YOU WILL NEED:
4 large firm pears
½ lemon
16 cloves
½ cinnamon stick
300 ml/½ pint red wine
2 tablespoons redcurrant jelly
4 orange slices
4 small fresh bay leaves, to decorate

Peel the pears, leaving the stalks intact; rub them all over with the lemon half to prevent discoloration. Stud each pear with 4 cloves.

Stand the pears upright in a pan; add the cinnamon stick, wine and just sufficient water to cover the pears. Bring to the boil and simmer gently until the pears are tender. Leave to cool in the cooking liquid.

Put 2 tablespoons of the cooking liquid into a small pan with the redcurrant jelly; bubble briskly for about 1 minute until the jelly has dissolved.

Place an orange slice on each of four small plates; drain the pears with a slotted spoon, and sit one on top of each orange slice. Spoon a little redcurrant glaze over each pear and decorate with a small bay leaf.

230 POACHED ORANGES WITH RAISINS

Preparation time:
20 minutes, plus cooling

Cooking time:
15 minutes

Serves 4

Calories:
160 per portion

YOU WILL NEED:
4 large oranges
300 ml/½ pint dry white wine
50 g/2 oz raisins
1 teaspoon powdered gelatine
2 tablespoons dry vermouth

Pare the rind from the oranges very thinly and cut it into fine matchstick strips. Put these into a saucepan with sufficient water to cover; bring to the boil and simmer for 4 minutes. Drain thoroughly and plunge the strips into a bowl of iced water.

Remove all the pith from the peeled oranges and put the fruit into a saucepan with the wine and raisins; simmer gently for 10 minutes, turning the oranges from time to time. Remove the oranges with a slotted spoon and place in a serving dish.

Dissolve the gelatine in the vermouth in a bowl over a saucepan of gently simmering water and stir into the cooking liquid; allow to cool and add half the orange rind strips. Spoon over the whole oranges, and scatter the remaining strips of rind around the oranges. Leave until completely cold.

COOK'S TIP

This recipe is based on a dessert which was very popular in the early 18th century when spices were extensively used. Cinnamon stick is the dried bark of a *species of laurel which flourishes in Sri Lanka.*

COOK'S TIP

The easiest way to remove any stubborn pieces of pith from an orange is with a clean razor blade in a suitable holder such as a craft knife.

231 STUFFED FIGS

Preparation time:	YOU WILL NEED:
15 minutes	12 *ripe fresh figs, preferably purple*
	ones
Serves 4	3 *tablespoons ground almonds*
Calories:	100 *g/4 oz fresh raspberries*
94 per portion	1 *tablespoon honey*
	4 *vine leaves, soaked in warm water*
	and dried, to serve

Snip off any excess stalk from each fig; make a criss-cross cut down from the stalk end and carefully ease the cut open.

Mix the ground almonds with the fresh raspberries and honey. Place a vine leaf, spread out flat, on each serving plate; arrange three figs on top of each one, and fill with the raspberry and almond purée.

232 MARINATED NECTARINES

Preparation time:	YOU WILL NEED:
25 minutes, plus	4 *large ripe nectarines*
chilling	1 *lemon*
	1 *large orange*
Serves 4	200 *ml/7 fl oz water*
Calories:	4 *tablespoons dry vermouth*
86 per portion	

Skin the nectarines (see Cook's Tip; peaches may be skinned the same way). Pare the skin from the lemon and cut into matchstick strips. Squeeze the lemon juice into a large bowl and fill up with iced water. Put the prepared nectarines into the lemon water.

Peel the orange thinly, removing all the pith; chop the flesh into pieces, discarding any pips. Cut the orange peel into matchstick strips. Put the orange flesh into a liquidizer with the water and vermouth; blend until smooth.

Lift the nectarines out of the lemon water and drain. Put the nectarines into a shallow dish and spoon over the prepared orange and vermouth sauce. Cover and chill for 2 hours. (No longer, otherwise the nectarines are likely to discolour.)

Sprinkle with the strips of lemon and orange peel and serve immediately.

COOK'S TIP

The stalk end of a ripe fig should feel slightly soft when pressed. If it is still hard, leave to ripen at room temperature.

COOK'S TIP

To skin a nectarine, nick the stalk end with a sharp knife and plunge the fruit into boiling water for 45 seconds. The skin will then slide off.

233 APRICOT AND BANANA COMPOTE

Preparation time:
15 minutes, plus
soaking and chilling

Serves 4

Calories:
130 per portion

YOU WILL NEED:
100 g/4 oz dried apricots
2 bananas
2 teaspoons lemon juice
25 g/1 oz raisins
150 ml/¼ pint natural low-fat yogurt
few drops of artificial liquid sweetener (optional)
grated nutmeg

Wash the apricots, put in a bowl and cover with cold water. Leave to soak overnight.

Slice the bananas and toss in the lemon juice. Place the apricots in a bowl with a little of the soaking liquid. Add the bananas and raisins, then divide the fruit between four glass serving dishes.

Sweeten the yogurt if preferred, spoon over the fruit and sprinkle with grated nutmeg. Chill before serving.

234 KIWI FRUIT SALAD

Preparation time:
25 minutes, plus
chilling

Serves 4

Calories:
119 per portion

YOU WILL NEED:
8 kiwi fruit
4 plump green grapes
8 plump black grapes
2 tablespoons dry white wine
2 tablespoons unsweetened orange juice

Peel the kiwi fruit and cut into thin slices; arrange these, overlapping, around the edges of four small plates. Skin the green grapes and halve the black ones.

Arrange the black grapes in the centre of each plate; place a whole green grape in the centre of this. Spoon the wine and the orange juice over and chill for 1 hour.

■ COOK'S TIP

Keep bananas at room temperature until they are sufficiently ripe to use. Take care when removing a banana from the 'hand' not to loosen the skin of the adjoining fruit. You can save time by using no-soak apricots in this recipe.

■ COOK'S TIP

Egg-shaped kiwi fruit with its brown hairy skin is now available most of the year. The fruit is ripe when it feels soft to the touch.

235 FRESH FRUIT SALAD

Preparation time:
25 minutes, plus
chilling

Cooking time:
4 minutes

Serves 8

Calories:
83 per portion

YOU WILL NEED:
2 tablespoons honey
120 ml/4 fl oz water
thinly pared rind and juice of 1 lemon
1 red dessert apple, quartered and
   cored
1 pear, quartered and cored
1 banana
1 small pineapple
2 oranges
100 g/4 oz black grapes, halved and
   seeded
100 g/4 oz strawberries, sliced

Put the honey, water and lemon rind in a small saucepan. Bring to the boil, simmer for 2 minutes, then strain and leave to cool. Stir in the lemon juice.

Slice the apple, pear and banana into a bowl, pour over the lemon syrup and stir to coat the fruit. Peel the pineapple with a sharp knife and cut the flesh into sections, discarding the central core. Peel the oranges, removing all pith, and divide into two segments. Add to the bowl with the pineapple, grapes and strawberries and mix.

Turn into a glass dish and chill until required.

236 CASSIS FRUIT SALAD

Preparation time:
30 minutes, plus
chilling

Serves 6

Calories:
118 per portion

YOU WILL NEED:
3 tablespoons unsweetened orange
   juice
4 tablespoons crème de cassis
2 tablespoons clear honey
450 g/1 lb black dessert cherries,
   stoned
225 g/8 oz ripe blackcurrants,
   trimmed and 'tailed'
225 g/8 oz loganberries or raspberries,
   hulled
2 tablespoons pine nuts

Mix together the orange juice, crème de cassis and honey and stir until the honey has dissolved. Mix the cherries, blackcurrants and berries. Pour over the cassis mixture, stir well, cover and chill for at least 3 hours. Some of the juice will be drawn from the fruit to make a tangy dressing.

Scatter on the pine nuts just before serving. Serve chilled, with natural low-fat yogurt.

▨ COOK'S TIP

It is essential to use fresh strawberries in this fruit salad but canned pineapple could be substituted for fresh if this is not available. Choose a variety which is canned in natural juice, not syrup.

▨ COOK'S TIP

In the soft fruit season, take advantage of pick-your-own opportunities to obtain high quality fruit at lower prices than charged in a shop.

237 BAKED FRUIT SALAD

Preparation time:
10 minutes

Cooking time:
20 minutes

Oven temperature:
200°C, 400°F, gas 6

Serves 4

Calories:
79 per portion

YOU WILL NEED:
1 grapefruit
2 oranges
1 eating apple, sliced
8 dried apricot halves
300 ml/½ pint unsweetened orange
juice

Slice the grapefruit and oranges, leaving on the peel. Put the grapefruit, orange and apple slices in a casserole with the apricots. Use the ends of the oranges and grapefruit to cover the tops.

Pour in the orange juice and cover with a lid or foil. Bake in the oven for about 20 minutes until all the fruit is soft. Discard the fruit ends. Serve hot or cold.

238 ROSY PEARS

Preparation time:
10 minutes

Cooking time:
30 minutes

Oven temperature:
200°C, 400°F, gas 6

Serves 4

Calories:
83 per portion

YOU WILL NEED:
4 large firm pears, peeled
250 ml/8 fl oz unsweetened orange
juice
120 ml/4 fl oz red wine
20-30 cardamom seeds, crushed
artificial liquid sweetener, to taste

Put the pears in an ovenproof dish and pour on the orange juice and red wine with the cardamom seeds. Bake in the oven for about 30 minutes until tender.

Taste the juice for sweetness and, if liked, add sweetener. Serve hot or chilled with the strained sauce.

▨ COOK'S TIP

Served hot, this nutritious dish is a healthy way to start breakfast on a cold morning. It is equally good served cold.

▨ COOK'S TIP

Cardamom seeds are strongly aromatic and can be used to flavour both sweet and savoury dishes. Choose a light red wine to cook the pears.

239 APPLE GATEAU

Preparation time:
20 minutes, plus
chilling

Cooking time:
20 minutes

Oven temperature:
190°C, 375°F, gas 5

Serves 4

Calories:
134 per portion

YOU WILL NEED:
2 teaspoons powdered gelatine
2 tablespoons water
*450 g/1 lb cooking apples, peeled,
    cored and sliced*
grated rind and juice of ½ lemon
artificial sweetener, to taste
1 egg yolk
4 tablespoons muesli cereal
25 g/1 oz low-fat spread
2 dessert apples, sliced
150 ml/¼ pint apple juice

Dissolve 1 teaspoon of the gelatine in the water in a bowl over
a saucepan of gently simmering water.

Poach the cooking apples with the lemon rind and juice and
a few tablespoons of water until tender. Add sweetener to
taste and beat in the egg yolk. Stir in the gelatine.

Bake the muesli in the oven for 8 minutes. Mix with the
low-fat spread while still hot. Spread the muesli over the base
of a loose-bottomed 18 cm/7 inch cake tin. Chill for 30
minutes.

Poach the dessert apple slices gently in the apple juice for
about 3 minutes; remove carefully and drain on absorbent
kitchen paper.

Dissolve the remaining gelatine in 2 tablespoons of the
apple juice in a bowl over a saucepan of gently simmering
water. Stir in the remaining apple juice.

Spread the apple purée over the muesli base; arrange the
apple slices on top. Spoon over the apple juice glaze and chill
for 4 hours.

▦ COOK'S TIP

*Most proprietary brands of
muesli contain some form of
sweetening. It is therefore
advisable to make your own
mixture by combining rolled
oats, wheat flakes, wheat*   *germ, a few chopped nuts
and some raisins.*

240 BAKED CRANBERRY PEARS

Preparation time:
25 minutes

Cooking time:
40 minutes

Oven temperature:
200°C, 400°F, gas 6

Serves 4

Calories:
134 per portion

YOU WILL NEED:
*4 large, ripe dessert pears, peeled but
    with the stalks in place*
*225 g/8 oz cranberries, thawed, if
    frozen*
1 tablespoon chopped hazelnuts
3 tablespoons clear honey
150 ml/¼ pint dry white wine
few drops of red food colouring
mint sprigs, to decorate

Working from the base and using a small teaspoon, scoop out
the pear cores. Chop 2 tablespoons of the cranberries and mix
with the nuts and 1 tablespoon of the honey. Press the mixture
into the pear cavities.

Put the remaining cranberries, honey, wine and a few drops
of red food colouring in a flameproof dish and bring to the
boil over a moderate heat. Simmer for 5 minutes. Stand the
pears upright in the dish and spoon the wine over them.

Cover the dish lightly with foil and cook in the oven for 30
minutes, basting the pears with the wine once or twice. Decorate each pear with a sprig of mint and serve hot or cold.

▦ COOK'S TIP

*The colour of honey
depends on the type of
flowers from which the bees
have collected nectar. For
example, acacia honey is a
very pale golden colour.*

241 RHUBARB AND RASPBERRY LAYER

Preparation time:
15 minutes, plus
chilling

Cooking time:
10-15 minutes

Serves 4

Calories:
161 per portion

YOU WILL NEED:
450 g/1 lb fresh rhubarb
225 g/8 oz fresh or frozen raspberries
50 g/2 oz soft brown sugar
225 g/8 oz low-fat soft cheese
150 ml/¼ pint natural low-fat yogurt
fresh raspberries or toasted almonds,
    to decorate

Wash and chop the rhubarb and put in a pan with the raspberries and sugar. Simmer for 10-15 minutes, until soft.

Blend in the cheese with the yogurt. Layer the fruit and yogurt mixture in four individual glass dishes. Chill for 2 hours. Decorate the pudding with raspberries or with toasted almonds before serving.

242 STRAWBERRY MOULD

Preparation time:
20 minutes, plus
setting

Serves 6

Calories:
68 per portion

YOU WILL NEED:
225 g/8 oz cottage cheese, sieved
150 ml/¼ pint natural low-fat yogurt
250 g/9 oz strawberries, puréed
3 teaspoons powdered gelatine
3 tablespoons water
3-4 drops of artificial liquid sweetener
2 egg whites
100 g/4 oz fresh sliced strawberries, to
    decorate

Mix together the cottage cheese, yogurt and strawberry purée.

Dissolve the gelatine in the water in a bowl over a pan of gently simmering water. Cool, then fold into the cheese mixture with sweetener to taste.

Whisk the egg whites until stiff and fold into the mixture. Pour into a 20 cm/8 inch loose-bottomed flan tin. Chill until set (about 3 hours).

Remove from the tin, place on a serving plate and decorate with the sliced strawberries.

▧ COOK'S TIP

Use a pair of sharp kitchen scissors to cut the rhubarb into even lengths. It is easier to avoid having any loose stringy bits when the rhubarb is cut in this way.

▧ COOK'S TIP

By sieving cottage cheese you can achieve a similar texture to curd cheese but with significantly fewer calories. First press out and discard any whey.

243 HONEY MINT FRUIT

Preparation time:
20 minutes, plus chilling

Cooking time:
20-25 minutes

Oven temperature:
180°C, 350°F, gas 4

Serves 4

Calories:
113 per portion

YOU WILL NEED:
8 dried apricots, chopped
2 dessert pears, peeled, cored and chopped
2 bananas, thickly sliced
2 red dessert apples, cored and sliced
2 pineapple rings, chopped
2 teaspoons lemon juice
2 tablespoons dry cider
2 teaspoons clear honey
12 mint leaves, finely chopped, or ½ teaspoon dried mint

Put all the fruit in a 1.2 litre/2 pint heatproof dish.

Mix together the lemon juice, cider and honey, then pour over the fruit. Stir in the mint and mix well. Cover and cook in the oven for 20-25 minutes. Chill slightly, then serve.

244 RASPBERRY FRUIT COCKTAIL

Preparation time:
15 minutes, plus standing and chilling

Serves 4

Calories:
83 per portion

YOU WILL NEED:
2 bananas
2 teaspoons lemon juice
2 peaches
25 g/1 oz raisins
4 tablespoons fresh orange juice
150 g/5 oz raspberries
a pinch of nutmeg

Peel and slice the bananas and brush the slices with lemon juice to prevent discoloration. Put in a bowl. Peel, stone and slice the peaches, then add to the bananas with the raisins. Add the orange juice and stir gently to mix. Leave for 30 minutes for the flavours to blend.

Divide the fruit between four individual glasses or dessert bowls.

Purée the raspberries by rubbing them through a sieve. Spoon a portion of raspberry purée over each serving of fruit to decorate and sprinkle with a pinch of nutmeg. Chill until ready to serve.

■ COOK'S TIP

Mint can be grown very successfully in a large pot either on a window sill or in the garden where it is more easily controlled this way.

■ COOK'S TIP

Most supermarkets now sell freshly squeezed orange juice in 500 ml/18 fl oz and 1 litre/1¾ pint bottles. It is much quicker to use this than to squeeze the fruit yourself. The juice can be stored in the refrigerator for several days.

245 LEMON YOGURT SYLLABUB

Preparation time:
15 minutes, plus
chilling

Serves 4

Calories:
174 per portion

YOU WILL NEED:
450 ml/¾ pint thick yogurt
1 tablespoon clear honey
grated rind of 1 lemon
juice of 2 lemons
2 tablespoons dry sherry
fresh fruit, to decorate

Whisk the yogurt in a bowl, then beat in the honey and lemon rind. Gradually add the lemon juice and sherry, stirring all the time.

Divide the mixture between four individual serving glasses. This syllabub is particularly delicious if served topped with a few fresh raspberries, strawberries or blackberries. Alternatively, decorate each glass with a thin slice of lemon and a sprig of mint. Serve chilled.

246 BLACKCURRANT FOOL

Preparation time:
20 minutes, plus
chilling

Cooking time:
15 minutes

Serves 4

Calories:
54 per portion

YOU WILL NEED:
1 tablespoon cornflour
300 ml/½ pint skimmed milk
few drops of artificial liquid sweetener
300 g/10 oz blackcurrants
1 tablespoon water
150 ml/¼ pint natural low-fat yogurt
few blackcurrants, to decorate

Blend the cornflour with a little of the milk. Heat the remaining milk and stir into the cornflour mixture, then return to the saucepan. Heat, stirring continuously until the mixture thickens. Cook for 1 minute. Add sweetener to taste and leave to cool.

Trim and wash the blackcurrants, then put in a pan with the water. Cook gently until the fruit is soft. Add sweetener to taste and leave to cool. Purée the fruit in a blender or rub through a sieve.

Add the fruit purée and yogurt to the sauce and whisk until well blended. Spoon into four individual serving dishes and decorate with blackcurrants. Chill before serving.

■ COOK'S TIP

Greek yogurt has quite a high fat content but you can make a yogurt of comparable consistency from skimmed long-life milk. This has already been heat-treated so it is not necessary to scald it before adding the culture. By adding skimmed milk powder to the milk you can make even thicker yogurt.

■ COOK'S TIP

If possible, use a blender to purée the blackcurrants rather than rubbing the fruit through a sieve as this reduces the fibre content which is mostly in the seeds.

247 ORANGE POTS

Preparation time:
15 minutes, plus
chilling

Cooking time:
5 minutes

Serves 4

Calories:
179 per portion

YOU WILL NEED:
4 teaspoons powdered gelatine
3 tablespoons fresh orange juice
350 g/12 oz curd cheese
3 tablespoons lemon juice
3 tablespoons skimmed milk
artificial liquid sweetener, to taste
4 orange slices

Dissolve the gelatine in the orange juice in a bowl over a saucepan of gently simmering water.

Blend the gelatine mixture with the remaining ingredients, adding sweetener to taste. Spoon into individual serving dishes and top each with a slice of orange.

248 BLACKBERRY SURPRISE

Preparation time:
20 minutes, plus
chilling

Cooking time:
7 minutes

Serves 6

Calories:
134 per portion

YOU WILL NEED:
450 g/1 lb blackberries
3 teaspoons clear honey
1 tablespoon lemon juice
2 teaspoons powdered gelatine
175 g/6 oz natural low-fat yogurt
4 Petit Suisse cheeses
2 egg whites
2 tablespoons port
1 tablespoon hazelnuts
2 slivers lemon rind, chopped

Place half the blackberries in a heavy-based saucepan over a gentle heat and stir until softened. Stir in 2 teaspoons of the honey. Remove from the heat, add the lemon juice and sprinkle in the gelatine, stirring well to dissolve. Rub through a sieve, then leave the mixture to cool and thicken.

Combine the yogurt and Petit Suisse cheeses and stir in the cooled blackberry purée. Whip the egg whites until stiff and fold in.

Reserve a few whole blackberries for decoration. Divide the remainder between six tall wineglasses and pour 1 teaspoon of port into each. Top up with the blackberry mixture and chill.

Just before serving, dry-fry the hazelnuts with the lemon rind. When evenly coloured, chop them and sprinkle a little over each glass. Decorate with the remaining berries and honey.

COOK'S TIP

This mixture makes an excellent dessert for a celebration picnic. Fill into individual plastic containers, top with a slice of orange and cover with a *lid or cling film. Transport to the picnic in a chill-bag.*

COOK'S TIP

Both cultivated and wild blackberries freeze extremely well. Just put the freshly picked fruit in a rigid plastic container and freeze.

249 ORANGE AND PINEAPPLE JELLY

Preparation time:	YOU WILL NEED:
10 minutes, plus setting	150 ml/¼ pint water
	1 packet orange jelly
Cooking time:	200 ml/7 fl oz unsweetened pineapple
3 minutes	juice
	150 ml/¼ pint natural low-fat yogurt
Serves 4	orange twists, to decorate
Calories:	
109 per portion	

Heat the water in a saucepan and add the jelly. Stir until dissolved, then add the pineapple juice. Pour into a bowl and place in the refrigerator until just beginning to set.

Whisk in the yogurt until well blended, then pour into four glass serving dishes. Leave until set, then decorate with orange twists.

250 APPLE RING WITH APRICOT SAUCE

Preparation time:	YOU WILL NEED:
30 minutes, plus soaking and setting	450 g/1 lb cooking apples, peeled, cored and chopped
	150 ml/¼ pint water
Cooking time:	grated rind and juice of 1 lemon
30 minutes	2 cloves
	25 g/1 oz powdered gelatine
Serves 6	2 eggs, separated
	40 g/1 ½ oz muscovado sugar
Calories:	150 ml/¼ pint low-fat yogurt
147 per portion	FOR THE SAUCE
	100 g/4 oz dried apricots
	300 ml/½ pint water
	rind and juice of ½ lemon
	½ cinnamon stick

Place the apples in a saucepan with the water, lemon rind and cloves. Bring to the boil and simmer for about 10 minutes. Discard the cloves.

Dissolve the gelatine in the lemon juice in a bowl over a saucepan of gently simmering water. Add to the apple mixture and blend in a liquidizer. Set aside to cool.

Whisk the egg yolks with the sugar until light and fluffy. Stir into the apple purée with the yogurt. Whisk the egg whites until stiff and fold into the purée. Rinse a 1.2 litre/2 pint ring mould with cold water. Pour in the apple mixture and chill 3 hours. Make the sauce (see Cook's Tip).

Turn the apple mould on to a serving dish, drizzle a little of the sauce over it and serve the remainder separately.

■ COOK'S TIP

Instead of a packet of orange jelly, you can use powdered gelatine with equal quantities of unsweetened orange and pineapple juices.

Vegetarians can use agar in similar proportions as a substitute for gelatine.

■ COOK'S TIP

Sauce: soak apricots in the water 2 hours. Add lemon rind, juice and cinnamon. Bring to boil, simmer 20 minutes. Remove cinnamon, purée the apricots.

251 RASPBERRY CHANTILLY

Preparation time:
15 minutes, plus
chilling

Serves 4

Calories:
102 per portion

YOU WILL NEED:
450 g/1 lb raspberries, hulled
1 tablespoon Grand Marnier
2 egg whites
150 g/5 oz quark
grated rind of ½ orange
1 tablespoon caster sugar
25 g/1 oz toasted flaked almonds, to
decorate

Divide the raspberries equally among four individual glasses
or dessert bowls, then spoon over the Grand Marnier. Cover
with cling film and chill until ready to serve.

Whisk the egg whites stiffly, then gently fold in the quark,
orange rind and sugar. Spoon the mixture over the raspberries
and decorate with the almonds. Serve immediately.

252 CURD CHEESE HEARTS

Preparation time:
20 minutes, plus
draining

Serves 4

Calories:
88 per portion

YOU WILL NEED:
225 g/8 oz cottage cheese, sieved
artificial liquid sweetener, to taste
150 ml/¼ pint natural low-fat yogurt
2 egg whites
1 tablespoon brandy
FOR THE DECORATION
tiny fresh vine leaves (if available)
small clusters of black grapes

Mix the cottage cheese with a little sweetener to taste (if you
do not have a very sweet tooth, this may not be necessary);
blend in the yogurt. Whisk the egg whites until stiff but not
dry; fold lightly but thoroughly into the cheese mixture together with the brandy.

Line four small perforated heart-shaped moulds with clean
muslin; spoon the cheese mixture into the lined moulds and
cover with another layer of muslin. Stand the moulds on a
baking tray with a rim, and chill for 6-8 hours; the excess
liquid should have drained away from the cheese, and the
moulds should be firm enough to turn out.

Unmould the hearts and decorate with vine leaves and clusters of grapes.

▨ COOK'S TIP

Quark is a soft white cheese
made from semi-skimmed
milk. It does not contain
salt. The fat content can
vary quite considerably so
to check the label.

▨ COOK'S TIP

If you do not have the
traditional moulds, make
holes in yogurt or cottage
cheese cartons and use these
in the same way.

253 BLUEBERRY CREAMS

Preparation time:
20 minutes, plus chilling

Cooking time:
20 minutes

Serves 4

Calories:
82 per portion

YOU WILL NEED:
3 tablespoons clear honey
2 tablespoons orange juice
1½ teaspoons grated orange rind
450 g/1 lb blueberries
3 tablespoons wholemeal flour
150 ml/¼ pint natural low-fat yogurt
4 small mint sprigs, to decorate

Put the honey, orange juice and orange rind into a saucepan and stir over a low heat until the honey has melted. Add the blueberries and simmer for 10 minutes, or until the fruit is tender. Purée the fruit and juice in a liquidizer, or rub them through a sieve.

Stir a little of the purée into the flour to make a smooth paste. Stir in the remaining purée, return it to the pan and stir over a medium heat until the purée thickens. Simmer for 3 minutes. Cool slightly, then divide the fruit purée between four individual serving glasses and chill for 2 hours.

Stir the yogurt through the blueberry purée and decorate with mint sprigs. Serve chilled.

254 STRAWBERRY AND ORANGE CHIFFON

Preparation time:
35-40 minutes, plus chilling

Serves 4

Calories:
90 per portion

YOU WILL NEED:
350 g/12 oz ripe strawberries
6 tablespoons orange juice
finely grated rind of ½ orange
1 tablespoon honey
2 eggs, separated
2 teaspoons powdered gelatine
2 tablespoons water
4 tablespoons natural low-fat yogurt

Reserve four whole strawberries for decoration. Put the remaining strawberries into a liquidizer and blend until smooth.

Put the orange juice and rind, honey and egg yolks into a bowl; whisk until thick, light and creamy.

Dissolve the gelatine in the water in a bowl over a saucepan of slightly simmering water.

Combine the strawberry purée and whisked egg yolk mixture, then stir in the dissolved gelatine and the yogurt. Leave until the mixture is about to set. Then whisk the egg whites until stiff but not dry and fold lightly but thoroughly into the strawberry mixture.

Spoon into individual glass dessert dishes and chill for 3 hours. Decorate each dessert with one of the reserved whole strawberries and serve.

▨ COOK'S TIP

Blueberries are known by a variety of other names including bilberries and whinberries in different parts of Britain. The fruit purée freezes well.

▨ COOK'S TIP

It is not necessary to use large, perfect strawberries for this dessert. Slightly over-ripe berries or the smaller ones known as jamming strawberries are *perfectly suitable. If you do not have a sweet tooth, omit the honey.*

255 RHUBARB AND GINGER FLUMMERY

Preparation time:
20 minutes, plus
setting

Cooking time:
12 minutes

Serves 4

Calories:
65 per portion

YOU WILL NEED:
*450 g/1 lb rhubarb, trimmed and
    chopped into rough lengths
grated rind and juice of ½ orange
¼ teaspoon ground ginger
3 tablespoons clear honey
2 teaspoons powdered gelatine
2 tablespoons water
2 egg whites*

Put the rhubarb into a saucepan with the orange rind and juice, ginger and honey. Simmer gently until the fruit is quite soft. Dissolve the gelatine in the water in a bowl over a saucepan of gently simmering water and add to the cooked rhubarb. Beat until smooth. Cool the rhubarb mixture until it is just on the point of setting.

Whisk the egg whites until stiff but not dry; fold lightly but thoroughly into the semi-set rhubarb mixture. Spoon into tall stemmed glasses. Chill until set.

256 ORANGE HONEY FLUFF

Preparation time:
10 minutes, plus
chilling

Serves 4

Calories:
65 per portion

YOU WILL NEED:
*25 g/1 oz honey
grated rind and juice of 1 orange
2 teaspoons lemon juice
300 ml/½ pint natural low-fat yogurt
2 egg whites
few strips of orange rind, to decorate*

Blend the honey with the orange and lemon juice. Stir in the grated orange rind and yogurt.

Whisk the egg whites until stiff and fold into the mixture. Spoon into four sundae dishes and decorate with the orange rind. Serve lightly chilled. Do not leave in the refrigerator for more than 1 hour or the mixture will start to separate.

■ COOK'S TIP

Rhubarb is the first home-grown fruit of the season to appear in the shops. Choose slender crisp stems for the best flavour. As the leaves are inedible, these should be carefully cut away with any portion of the crown or root.

■ COOK'S TIP

Remember to take the egg whites out of the refrigerator 30 minutes before you whisk them. This will help to increase their bulk.

257 RASPBERRY AND YOGURT ICE CREAM

Preparation time:
10 minutes, plus freezing

Serves 4

Calories:
206 per portion

YOU WILL NEED:
225 g/8 oz fresh raspberries
50 g/2 oz icing sugar
2 tablespoons clear honey
2 tablespoons lemon juice
900 ml/1½ pints natural low-fat yogurt
sprigs of fresh salad burnet (if available), to decorate

If freezing the ice cream in the refrigerator set at its lowest temperature. Liquidize the raspberries, then rub them through a sieve. Add all the other ingredients, stir well and freeze as fast as possible either in the freezing compartment of the refrigerator or in the freezer. Scoop the ice cream into glasses and decorate each serving with a sprig of salad burnet.

258 PEACH GRANITA

Preparation time:
15 minutes, plus freezing

Cooking time:
6 minutes

Serves 4

Calories:
69 per portion

YOU WILL NEED:
350 g/12 oz fresh ripe peaches
150 ml/¼ pint dry white wine
150 ml/¼ pint fresh orange juice
2 egg whites

Remove the skin from each peach (see Recipe 232). Halve the fruit, removing the stones, and chop the flesh roughly.

Put the peach flesh into a saucepan with the white wine and orange juice. Simmer gently for 5 minutes. Then blend the peaches and the liquid in a liquidizer until smooth. Leave to cool. Put the mixture into a shallow container; freeze until the granita is 'slushy' around the edges, then tip into a bowl and break up the ice crystals. Whisk the egg whites until stiff but not dry; fold lightly but thoroughly into the partly-frozen granita. Return to the container and re-freeze for 2-3 hours until firm.

■ COOK'S TIP

The young leaves of garden or salad burnet taste and smell rather like cucumber which is why they were once much used in wine cups.

■ COOK'S TIP

This type of iced dessert is very refreshing on a hot summer day. The peaches and fresh orange juice provide enough natural sweetness to make it *unnecessary to use any artificial sweetener.*

259 WHOLE STRAWBERRY ICE CREAM

Preparation time:	YOU WILL NEED:
15 minutes, plus freezing	*3 egg yolks*
	1 tablespoon redcurrant jelly
	1 tablespoon red vermouth
Serves 4	*300 ml/½ pint natural low-fat yogurt*
Calories:	*350 g/12 oz ripe strawberries, hulled*
79 per portion	*8 strawberries with stalks, halved, to decorate*

Put the egg yolks into a blender with the redcurrant jelly, vermouth, yogurt and half the strawberries; blend until smooth. Transfer the mixture to a shallow container, and freeze until the ice cream starts to harden around the edges.

Tip the ice cream into a bowl and beat to break up the ice crystals. Chop the remaining strawberries and mix into the semi-set ice cream. Return to the container and freeze until quite firm. Scoop the ice cream into stemmed glasses and decorate each one with strawberry halves.

260 COFFEE SORBET

Preparation time:	YOU WILL NEED:
5 minutes, plus freezing	*600 ml/1 pint natural low-fat yogurt*
	4 tablespoons skimmed milk powder
Serves 4	*4 teaspoons instant coffee powder or granules*
Calories:	*artificial liquid sweetener, to taste*
99 per portion	

Mix the yogurt, skimmed milk powder and instant coffee together. Add artificial sweetener to taste and stir well.

Pour into a shallow dish and freeze for 2-3 hours. Stir occasionally, mixing the frozen edges to the centre. The mixture should be eaten when quite soft.

◼ COOK'S TIP

Strawberries should be kept in the refrigerator or a cool place if not being eaten immediately. The fruit should be washed before it is hulled.

◼ COOK'S TIP

The skimmed milk powder gives a deliciously smooth texture to the sorbet and helps to prevent the mixture freezing too hard. If you do not use an artificial *sweetener in coffee, you will not need to add any to the sorbet!*

DRINKS

When on a slimming diet it is particularly important to maintain a good intake of fluids and long, refreshing drinks can also help to ward off hunger pangs! A blender is invaluable in creating vitamin-packed fruit and vegetable cocktails, or whisking nutritious drinks such as Breakfast in a Glass which can equally well be drunk at other times of the day. Low-alcohol or non-alcoholic drinks and fruit cups and punches are always popular with slimmers, drivers and the health-conscious.

261 SAN FRANCISCO

Preparation time:
5 minutes

Serves 4

Calories:
101 per portion

YOU WILL NEED:
175 ml/6 fl oz unsweetened orange juice
175 ml/6 fl oz unsweetened lemon juice
175 ml/6 fl oz unsweetened pineapple juice
175 ml/6 fl oz unsweetened grapefruit juice
4 dashes grenadine
4 egg whites
soda water, to top up
slice of fruit, to decorate

Shake all the ingredients, except the soda water, together well, and strain into a 1 litre/2 pint jug. Top up with soda water. Pour into individual glasses to serve. To decorate the glasses, spear thin slices of fruit on to cocktail sticks. Serve the drinks with straws.

262 GREEN SUMMER COOLER

Preparation time:
5 minutes

Serves 4

Calories:
25 per portion

YOU WILL NEED:
4 tablespoons crème de menthe
crushed ice
1.2 litres/2 pints sparkling mineral water
mint sprigs, to garnish

Put a teaspoonful of the crème de menthe in the bottom of four tall glasses. Add a little crushed ice, top up with sparkling mineral water and serve immediately garnished with mint sprigs.

◾ COOK'S TIP

Store citrus fruit in the crisper drawer of the refrigerator. Always taste any food or drink after it has been chilled as chilling can affect quite markedly the amount of flavouring or sweetening required.

◾ COOK'S TIP

You can use a special gadget which crushes ice in a lidded container or put ice cubes in a strong polythene bag and smash them with a wooden mallet.

263 TOMATO JUICE

Preparation time:
15 minutes, plus
chilling

Serves 4

Calories:
26 per portion

YOU WILL NEED:
500 g/1¼ lb ripe tomatoes, peeled and
    roughly chopped
1 teaspoon salt
1 teaspoon lemon juice
1 teaspoon soft brown sugar
1 teaspoon Worcestershire sauce
300 ml/½ pint water
1 teaspoon tomato purée
pepper
FOR THE GARNISH
4 mint sprigs
4 lemon slices

Put all the ingredients, with pepper to taste, in a blender and
blend for 30 seconds. Rub through a sieve to remove the
seeds, then chill for about 2 hours.

Pour the tomato juice into glasses and garnish with mint
sprigs and lemon slices to serve.

264 PINK TONIC

Preparation time:
2 minutes

Serves 4

Calories:
6 per portion

YOU WILL NEED:
1 litre/1¾ pints low-calorie tonic
    water
few drops of angostura bitters
ice cubes

Divide the tonic water between four glasses and stir a few
drops of angostura bitters into each glass. Add ice cubes and
serve immediately.

▌ COOK'S TIP

*If you have a surplus of ripe
tomatoes at the peak of
their growing season, turn
some into tomato juice.
Vary the flavour subtly by
using celery or garlic salt.*

▌ COOK'S TIP

*Make decorative ice cubes
to float in summer drinks.
Put a pink rose petal in
each section of an ice tray,
fill with water and freeze.*

265 TENDERBERRY

Preparation time:
10 minutes

Serves 4

Calories:
79 per portion

YOU WILL NEED:
450 g/1 lb strawberries, hulled
2 tablespoons fresh orange juice
450 ml/¾ pint natural low-fat yogurt
crushed ice
450 ml/¾ pint low-calorie dry ginger
*   ale*
red food colouring
ground ginger

Reserve 4 strawberries. Put the remaining strawberries, orange juice and yogurt in a blender with some crushed ice and blend on maximum speed for 30 seconds. Divide between four tumblers. Add the dry ginger ale and a little red food colouring and stir. Sprinkle a little ginger on top and decorate each glass with one of the reserved strawberries.

266 SUMMER CUP

Preparation time:
5 minutes, plus
chilling

Cooking time:
5 minutes

Serves 8

Calories:
113 per portion

YOU WILL NEED:
450 g/1 lb raspberries
1 tablespoon water
600 ml/1 pint sparkling mineral water
1 x 750 ml/1¼ pints bottle sparkling
*   dry white wine*
2 tablespoons crème de cassis

Crush the raspberries with the back of a wooden spoon and put them in a saucepan with the tablespoon of water; bring to boiling point and simmer for 3 minutes.

Cool, then combine with the other ingredients and put in an airtight container. Refrigerate overnight.

Strain the cup before serving.

■ COOK'S TIP

Red-skinned Victoria plums can be used as an alternative to the strawberries to make an equally delicious summer drink. Try sprinkling a little *cinnamon on top of each glass instead of the ground ginger.*

■ COOK'S TIP

The strained cup can be poured into a chilled vacuum flask for a picnic. As an alternative to the crème de cassis, try crème de framboise.

267 TEA, RUM AND ORANGE PUNCH

Preparation time:
20 minutes

Serves 8

Calories:
94 per portion

YOU WILL NEED:
10 oranges
2 litres/3 ½ pints hot tea, not too
strong
2 lemons
1 cinnamon stick
120 ml/4 fl oz dark rum
artificial sweetener, to taste

Peel a very thin layer of skin from one of the oranges and steep it in the freshly made hot tea. Squeeze the juice out of all the fruit except one half orange and one half lemon. Strain both juices and heat gently with the cinnamon stick.

Slice the half orange and half lemon as thinly as possible and soak the slices in the rum. When the orange and lemon juice reaches boiling point stir it into the tea, add the rum with the fruit slices. Taste, and stir in artificial sweetener to taste, if liked. Remove the rind and cinnamon stick before serving.

268 BREAKFAST IN A GLASS

Preparation time:
15 minutes, plus
soaking and chilling

Cooking time:
10-12 minutes

Serves 4

Calories:
266 per portion

YOU WILL NEED:
75 g/3 oz porridge oats
300 ml/½ pint skimmed milk
2 large cooking apples, peeled, cored
and chopped
grated rind of 1 orange
juice of 2 oranges
300 ml/½ pint buttermilk, chilled
2 tablespoons honey
2 eggs
2 tablespoons jumbo oats

Put the porridge oats and skimmed milk in a bowl, cover and leave to soak overnight in the refrigerator.

Put the apple, orange rind, reserving a few strands, and orange juice into a small saucepan, bring to the boil and simmer for 10 minutes, or until the apple is tender. Set aside to cool, then chill overnight.

The following morning put the porridge oats, milk, apple, buttermilk, honey and eggs in a blender and liquidize.

Divide the drink between four glasses, sprinkle the jumbo oats and reserved orange rind on top and serve immediately.

■ COOK'S TIP

Tea may be considered the national drink of Britain but it is only rarely used as an ingredient. A flowery orange pekoe would be particularly suitable here.

■ COOK'S TIP

If you and your family are tempted to skip breakfast in the rush to get ready in the morning, try serving this nutritious drink. It will help to stave off those mid- *morning hunger pangs.*

INDEX